Finding My Father

Jim Pennington

Printed in the United States of America

First Printing: 2018

Print ISBN: 978-1-54395-097-7
eBook ISBN: 978-1-54395-098-4

Firefall Media
www.firefallinternational.org

Cover art by Jason Flack

This book is dedicated to Nancy, my faithful and loving wife who has shown me true, sacrificial love as we follow Jesus together. She has encouraged and inspired me to deeper love, greater faith and more fruitful service. It is also dedicated to our three daughters, Hannah, Abby and Grace. They have given me the joy of being a father. What a delight they are to my heart!

TABLE OF CONTENTS

CHAPTER ONE
AT SEVENTEEN

I watched in disbelief as my father's casket was lowered into the grave. My mind struggled with the thoughts. I was forced to conclude, "This is not a bad dream. This is real. My father is gone. I don't have a Dad anymore." I tried to reason my way through the confusion. "It's O.K. I'm seventeen years old. I'm old enough to make it. I'll be fine." But I wasn't fine. A dark emptiness settled into my soul fueled by grief, remorse, the sickness of unfulfilled hopes, and the shame of unmet expectations. Dad was gone and nothing I could do would change that. But I was only 17.

Two weeks earlier, after returning from Scout camp I had helped Dad spread gravel on the steep driveway to the lake house. We had two houses, one in town and one on the lake. It was only a four-mile drive between the two, but they seemed to be worlds apart. Every summer our family would move to the lake house where my days were filled with swimming, skiing, sailing or putting around the lake to see friends in my small motorboat. I wore a swimsuit or cut-off jean shorts. No shoes, no shirt required. I did get a thrill once when my bare foot stepped on a hidden green snake. I don't know which one of us moved faster.

My skin was tanned and my curly hair bleached blond by the sun. The road leading to the lake house was a steep one descending sharply, and often rutted by rain. A couple of times a year we had to fill in the ruts with gravel to slow the erosion and keep the road drivable. So, Dad and I spent a hot June Sunday afternoon filling the ruts and spreading the gravel on the road. It was hard work, but we were both used to hard work. It was a virtue in my family. Maybe the highest virtue of all.

Monday morning came, and Dad did something that I had never known him to do before. He went to see the doctor. I thought my Dad was indestructible. Sure, he smoked like a chimney and drank like a fish. He took a break from work most days for donuts and coffee in the morning or pie and coffee in the afternoon next door to our clothing store at the Blue Bell Café, but I never saw it coming. Not in a million years.

The doctor told him, "Penny, you've had a heart attack," and put him into the hospital. Two weeks later he had a second heart attack and in a matter of hours, he was gone. I was left with a part of my life that I thought would never be filled again. I had a soul-deep ache that I thought might never go away.

Growing Up Country, Growing Up Poor

My Dad didn't talk a lot about how he grew up. Maybe it was a generational thing. Reflection and self-analysis weren't high on the list. But from what I can piece together, he grew up poor. I mean really poor. Country poor. The kind of poor that would make the senior class president quit school to help earn money for the family.

He was born in 1908, "aught eight," he used to say. I think it's supposed to be "naught eight," but like I said, it was country. As he was growing up in rural Arkansas, so was a mechanized America. Cars were replacing the horse and buggy. Telegraph and telephone would change communication and the airplane was not far behind transforming world travel and how wars were fought. Dad was at home in this newly mechanized world learning the intricacies of compression and carburetion, camshaft rotation and cylinder pressure. He mastered basic electronics. He was a dang good mechanic, kept a steady job but lived on the wild side. The first time my mother saw him, he was driving one of those early Ford models down the highway. He was sitting on top of the seat. Not in the seat, on top of it, steering with his feet with his upper body sticking above the windshield. People warned her about seeing that "wild Pennington boy," but who can explain love. They married and moved to Hot Springs, the town where I grew up. Dad went to work for his father-in-law, M. L. Stueart, managing a grocery store, the Stueart Store Number 1.

Millard Luther Stueart

My grandfather, M. L. Stueart or "Uncle Millard" to his customers, owned the general store in a small community where two railroad lines crossed. The name of the town was Tokio, Arkansas (pronounced like the Japanese city) but the locals just called it Toki. Uncle Millard raised cattle, developed peach orchards and ran a profitable general store, at least until the Depression hit. He was doing credit business with a lot of outflow and not enough income. He had a wife, three daughters and a son to look after. I get the idea that mediocrity never worked for M. L. Stueart. In 1932 he sold what he could, went to the big city of Hot Springs and started over in the grocery business.

It was a hard start. Hot Springs was a corrupt town. Gangsters and dirty politicians were in league with dirty cops, and everybody had their hands out. You didn't just come into Hot Springs and start up some kind of business. Threats were made, tires were slashed, and vandalism was a common occurrence. But in time Millard made it, and he made it big. In his heyday there were fourteen Stueart Stores spread all around Hot Springs. They were the dominant grocery chain with a huge warehouse and a wholesale business that covered several counties. The family remained at the home place in Toki with Millard traveling back and forth. In 1934 he moved his family to Hot Springs. He brought several other men, then young men, from Toki to Hot Springs to work for him. In time, they too became wealthy businessmen and community leaders.

Living the American Dream

So after Mom and Dad were married, Dad ran the Number 1 Stueart Store, downtown next to the courthouse. Mom was a beautician, what they called a "beauty operator" back then. Her shop was down the street. Often, they would meet for lunch at the Pappas Brothers restaurant. This Greek family had invented a dish they called the "Three-Way," a bowl of chili, beans and pasta. Mom and Dad could each have a "Three-Way" and a Coca-Cola (or maybe an R.C. Cola, the R.C. stood for Royal Crown) for a quarter. They always liked to tell me how little they paid for stuff back then. The "Three-Way" was still around when I was growing up and I ate my share of them, but I can't tell you what it cost.

Life was good in America until Hitler started invading the nations of Europe and Japan bombed Pearl Harbor, then all hell broke loose. All the young men were joining the armed forces to fight the war. It was a shame to be drafted, downright unpatriotic. I grew up knowing which men in my neighborhood had to be drafted. Dad was too old to be drafted, but he joined the Air Force anyway. Back then it was called the Army Air Corps. His aptitude for engines and motors came to the fore. (He always told me an engine is internal combustion and a motor is electrical. I think that distinction's been lost but I can't ever get past it. My apologies go to all the motorheads).

He was trained as an airplane mechanic and sent to serve in India. I don't think he'd ever been out of Arkansas before. I can't imagine the culture shock. I know he got sick and that skinny Arkansas boy got even skinnier and his skin turned yellow. But like the men of that generation, he made the best of it. Humor and grit seemed to take these men a long way. They were tough, hard scrabble, determined and unrelenting. If they had weaknesses, they didn't let them show. Light another cigarette, pour another drink and get on with it. Dream about pin-up girls and don't think too much about the ones you love back home. That could get a guy down real quick. There's a job to do, a war to fight, a world to save. And, by golly, they did it.

They were welcomed home as the heroes they were. Dad did tell me about his first meal in America after getting off the boat in New Jersey, before taking the troop train home to Arkansas. It was a fat greasy hamburger and a milkshake. That's what he wanted. A hamburger and a milkshake. It seems strange to me writing this while sitting in an apartment in China, but from here I can see that so much of my Dad's life was essential Americana. He lived the American dream. He hit it at the right time. It was the time of American Idealism at its peak. America and her allies had won the war, and everybody knew America had carried the lion's share. The economy was on an upswing. Heck, it was booming. Everything was possible with ingenuity, determination and hard work.

Back in Hot Springs, things began to change. The returning G.I.'s decided to do something about the mobsters and corruption, and elected their own officials who remained in office for decades. Dad went back into the grocery business for a while. I'm just guessing here, but it's probably not so easy to work for your father-in-law when you're convinced you can do anything you set your mind to. There may have been some intervening businesses. I know somewhere along the way Dad learned how to repair radios and television sets (back when people repaired them instead of throwing them away). He also picked up carpentry and cabinet making. Most boys think that their dads can do anything. Mine could. I remember once when the air conditioning unit in the business quit working. Three successive service men came to rehabilitate the unit to no avail. My Dad didn't get mad often, but this time I could smell the smoke and see the steam. He disassembled the unit and removed the defective part. For some unknown reason I went with him to the service desk of the utility company (they were responsible for servicing the units).

He slammed the part down on the counter and in a barely restrained voice explained exactly how to fix it. It got fixed.

Eventually Dad and my uncle started Oaklawn Hardware Store as a joint venture. It really was more than a hardware store. They sold appliances, bicycles, guns and sporting goods, as well as the normal hardware fare. Uncle Dick was one of a kind. He had spent about a year in a German P.O.W. camp after the bomber he was piloting was shot down over Austria. He never smoked cigars, but he was always chewing one. His hearing wasn't so good and instead of saying, "what?" or "excuse me?" or, God forbid, "pardon me?" He would say, "Stepped in what?" He was tall and skinny and hunched over. Maybe his posture came from an injury from the plane crash or the imprisonment, but he never talked about it. He never talked about the war, the prison camp or the mental strain.

Dad decided to part ways with Dick and start his own business. The payout from Dick was the small Duracraft motorboat I used to cruise the lake. In 1953, Oaklawn Sportswear was born. It started as a source for sports clothing (football and basketball uniforms, swimwear, golf outfits) but soon grew into more profitable sales of all kinds of casual and dress clothing. The store carried everything from Levi jeans to business suits on the men's side and both casual and dress clothing for women. If my parents could sell it, they'd stock it. One hot item for the ladies was purses with fake precious stones of various colors glued on. The stones would make up the images of animals and birds like peacocks and tigers. Dad was forever gluing back on the stones that came loose in shipping. They used to say, "There's no accounting for taste." Predicting fashion trends was risky, but my folks were pretty good at it and made good money. My life growing up revolved around working in the family business. My understanding of life and how it worked came through the filter of customer service, attention to detail, making a good impression and success through hard work. The goal of continual improvement was more than a business concept. It was our lifestyle.

1953 was a big year in my family. Oaklawn Sportswear came into being, a new Pontiac car with a Straight 8 engine and the family's first television set were purchased, and I was born. My brother, Stueart, had been born in 1947. A camp director I once worked for told me that there are no problem children, only children with problems. If that's true, Stueart was a child with problems. He had problems with rules, he had problems with authority and discipline, he had problems with respecting others and, believe it or not, he had problems with me. He put a sign on his bedroom door for my benefit, "DON'T GO AWAY MAD, JUST GO AWAY." Stueart was mad a lot. He was in trouble a lot, and he smarted-off a lot which got him into more trouble. Trouble was a lifestyle. He was likable, popular, funny, but never met a boundary he wouldn't cross. The crazy thing is, he seemed to always get caught. He could never get away with anything. He would sneak out in the second car when Mom and Dad were out at night and run out of gas. He would leave beer in the trunk of the car when he was underage, and Dad would find it when he opened the trunk to load up his golf clubs. He and his friends were fooling around in an abandoned house and ended up burning it to the ground, alerting the authorities. That was one of the times the police brought him home. That was Stueart. So, when I came along and as I grew up there was a hope for a well-behaved, compliant child. I filled that role and became Dad's favorite.

CHAPTER TWO
LET'S PLAY GOLF

Like most of the businessmen and professionals in my town, my father played golf. Our family membership at the Hot Springs Golf and Country Club was as important as our membership at the First Methodist Church. They both served as symbols of our status in the community, as well as providing tangible benefits. During my teenage years, Dad started taking me to play golf with him. He saw in me the potential to excel at the sport; he even told me that he thought I could become a professional golfer. I really liked the water sports like swimming and skiing, but golf was O.K., too, for a while. We would put on our golf outfits, get our clubs and shoes and drive out Malvern Road to the Country Club.

What, in my mind, could have been a fun father–son outing soon turned into something very different. Golf is a game of nuances and Dad was always teaching, adjusting, and perfecting my golf game. "Change your stance; your feet need to be farther apart. Move your right hand farther over when you grip the club. Keep your head down. Don't bend your elbow. Follow through when you swing." The expected fun day on the links turned out to be an exercise in futility. The harder I tried, the more mistakes I made. The more mistakes I made, the more nervous I became. His corrections sounded like condemnations. Every shot of every hole showed me that I didn't measure up to his standard. By the end of the day, I felt like a failure. It's wasn't that I had played a bad round of golf. When I played with my friends some days were better than others, but I shot pretty well. This was different. I didn't feel that it was an off day, or that there was room for improvement in my golf game. It was more than that. It wasn't even that I had failed to please my dad on that day. It went beyond what I had done to who I was. I hadn't just failed. I *was* a failure.

Two Perspectives

Those corrections on the fairways and greens were pieces of a much larger mosaic. Dad had such high expectations for me that he invested his hopes in the person I would become. He had it tough growing up. I had it much easier. In his mind, that gave me a platform for much greater success. He could see me as a person with wealth and influence, possessing everything this world had to offer. He saw it as his obligation as a father to push me to higher achievement. I think his disappointment with my brother, Stueart, caused his emotional investment in my success to be amplified. No opportunity was missed to instruct me, correct me, and guide me to the promised land of the American Dream, Part Two. I worked dutifully at the family business. I made good grades in school. I worked my way through the ranks in Scouting. I worked for a year with the pastor of my church to earn the Boy Scout's "God and Country Award," and I was invited to join the Order of the Arrow, an honorary organization within the Boy Scouts of America. I knew Dad was proud of me when I was honored for an accomplishment, but it never seemed to be enough. It seemed like when I would meet his expectations, he would raise the bar. I wasn't conscious of this pattern, but I was aware of a growing discontent. Whatever I did, it didn't seem to be enough. That unfulfilled ache just kept coming up.

I could never satisfy my father.

From his perspective, he had one son who had the potential to exceed his own success in life. Someone who, if motivated and guided, could complete advanced degrees, go into a lucrative profession, make enough money to be secure and happy and live life on his own terms. I can understand now that his motive was love, as he understood it, and hope for a better life, as he defined it.

My perspective was much different.

I felt a growing weight of disappointment. His corrections sounded to me like condemnations. His "adjustments" were, to my ears, judgments declaring me a failure in his eyes. At some point, I gave up. I quit trying. It didn't happen all at once. There was no critical juncture of turning and walking away. There was no straw that broke the camel's back. But by my mid-teen years, I quit trying to please my father because I felt that whatever I did was not enough.

Maybe it was a defense mechanism. Maybe I was justifying my own frustrations. But I started to resent my father. I resented some of the things he did, and I resented some of his values. To be honest, I let my resentment extend to him as a person, the way I feared his disappointment went beyond what I did to who I was. Dad was an alcoholic. He stayed sober enough to run his business successfully and work as a community leader. He served as President of a civic club and was on the church's Board of Trustees. He would drink after hours or when Mom was away on buying trips. He would binge drink when he could work it in, but he was never far from a bottle or far from being drunk. I resented his alcoholism. I resented the embarrassment I felt when we were in public and he was drunk. He thought he could handle it. Maybe he could, but I couldn't. I guess I started drinking when I was 14 or 15. I'm not sure of my age, but I am sure of this: When I drank, I drank to get drunk. I resented what he did, but I was going down the same road.

Our family life revolved around "the store." I suppose other people who have grown up in a family business know this dynamic. Dinner conversation around meals, if the TV was turned down, centered on who had not paid their bill, and how they had the money, and what was wrong with them that they wouldn't do what they should do. Some nights Dad would read the World Book Encyclopedia. He would just pick a volume, pick an article and start reading. Or he would read the latest edition of National Geographic. He was a life-long learner. But most nights he would sit in his easy chair and watch TV until he fell asleep.

That's the pattern that I remember. Get up in the morning, go to work, come home, eat supper, watch TV and fall asleep. I held a growing resentment that the goal of his life was to make money to buy houses, cars, boats, Country Club memberships and vacations, and to build retirement savings. In my mind, while enjoying the benefits of this income, I concluded that it didn't seem to help him and Mom get along, or help my relationship with him, or do any good beyond our personal consumption. Just like Dad had been shaped by his generation, I was being shaped by mine. And what a generation it was.

The Sixties

This was the 1960s. The nation was in a violent vortex of cultural change. President Johnson had called out the National Guard sixty miles away in Little Rock to allow a "Negro" student to attend Central High School. Arkansas' racist governor Orval Faubus had vowed that colored students (that was the "nice" word) would not attend high school with whites. In Alabama, dogs and high-pressure water hoses had been used against the peaceful protests of blacks. Everywhere in the South, the Ku Klux Klan terrorized and murdered with impunity. Vietnam was a quagmire that divided the nation. Protesters were treated violently at the 1968 Democratic National Convention in Chicago. Four college students were gunned down by National Guard troops at Kent State University in Ohio. The peace and love idealism of Haight-Ashbury in San Francisco and Woodstock in New York had been fractured and some of the splinter movements traded flowers for bombs. The Black Panthers advocated race war, the Weather Underground (taking their name from the Bob Dylan lyric, "you don't need a weatherman to know which way the wind blows") planned to bring down the government, or as it was better known, "the military-industrial complex."

Chet Huntley and David Brinkley, the newscasters of the day, brought these dramatic events into our home every evening on the nightly news. Dad and I watched the same stories but formed very different conclusions. I had grown up with a racist mentality. We had a black (we would have said, "negro") maid named Hertasena, we just called her Sena. My parents gave her husband a new "preachin' suit" every year. But I learned early the difference between black (or "colored") and white. "If you find a Coke bottle with some Coke still in it, don't drink it. A colored person might have been drinking out of it." Tokio, Arkansas, where my mother grew up, had "Sundowner Laws." These required all colored people to be out of town by sundown because everyone thought they couldn't be trusted and it was hard to see them at night. (Yes, as disgusting as it sounds, I was really told that). My Dad seriously thought that Woodstock was a communist training camp disguised as a music festival. McCarthy had been right. There were all kinds of communist plots to overthrow the American government and part of the Russian plan was to brainwash the young people to join the revolution. I didn't need any Russian help. I had Bob Dylan and Joan Baez, Crosby, Stills, Nash and Young. I knew the times they were a changing. In my naiveté, swept up in the music and revolution of the day, compounded by the distance I felt from my father, I rejected his values. In my teenage simplicity, it seemed easy to take the next step and reject him.

Looking back, I think most of this journey for me was internal. I was thankful that Dad was never an angry drunk. I wasn't combative, either. (Unlike my brother who once tried to throw punches at Dad. Dad just deflected them and restrained Stueart until he calmed down). I reasoned that in a few years, when I finished college, I would change, get my life together and then Dad would be proud of me. But he had to feel it. He must have discerned the growing distance. He must have seen the rebellion he despised in society working its way into the psyche of his son. I don't know for sure, but under the drive to succeed and the drunken binges, it must have broken his heart.

And then he died.

Maybe it wasn't the gravel that Sunday on the driveway that killed him. Maybe it wasn't the cigarettes and alcohol and poor diet that killed him. Maybe he just gave up.

When I watched his casket go down in the grave I realized that it was too late to restore what had been broken. It was too late to regain what had been lost. Dad was gone. I felt remorse and grief that I had lost my father, but there was a weight that hung on my soul that, if it could have been measured, surely exceeded the weight of grief.

It was the weight of shame and disappointment that I had failed to meet his expectations.

He carried such high hopes for me to be his legacy and his redemption. I had failed my father. I *was* a failure. That night after the funeral, I took my first psychedelic drugs. It was a bad trip where giant flowers turned into snakes and spiders. My life was becoming a bad trip.

CHAPTER THREE
WHAT A LONG, STRANGE TRIP IT'S BEEN

My father died during the summer between my senior year in high school and my freshman year at college. I had been accepted at a prestigious liberal arts college that maintained an affiliation with the United Methodist Church. After Dad died, I contracted mononucleosis. That summer I remember being weak, depressed, waiting to go to college and smoking a lot of pot. Marijuana had found its way into my town and into my hands during my senior year of high school. I jumped on the bandwagon early and became a supplier for my friends and for people who wanted to be my friends because I had dope.

I spent time sitting in parking lots, listening to music and becoming an expert on which bands were groovy. I knew all the albums by the big names like Beatles, Rolling Stones, Grateful Dead, The Band and Jimi Hendrix. I also knew a lot of obscure bands that I could pull out to impress my friends. They had names like Hot Tuna, Mott the Hoople, Procol Harum and Spirit. One of my buddies lost his leg in a motorcycle accident. I think we'd been smoking together just before the wreck. College would be better. It would be intellectually stimulating with the freedom to live life as it came. I was really happy when I packed up my blue Plymouth Road Runner. The car had been a gift from Dad. He told me that if I made good grades and stayed out of jail, he'd buy me any kind of car I wanted on my seventeenth birthday. My brother had the same opportunity, but he didn't get to collect. Off I went with my stereo, my stash and a few clothes to Hendrix College (no relation to Jimi).

Hendrix, But Not Jimi

My freshman year at Hendrix was a year of exploration and experimentation. Some of it took place in the classroom or through the assigned readings, but most of my experimentation took place in darkened rooms under the unnatural glow of black light posters, smoking, snorting, dropping or chewing something new. I told myself that I'd never use the needle. Neil Young had warned in his song "The Needle and the Damage Done" that "every junkie's like a setting sun." I kept my promise to myself and never used heroine or shot anything else. Even though I preferred psychedelic drugs, I tried to stay away from LSD because of the potential chromosomal damage, but you never knew for sure what you were getting.

Once I bought what I thought was Psilocybin, a drug derived from the Peyote cactus. The seller got busted minutes after I made my buy and when the drug was analyzed it turned out to be almost pure cocaine. I guess he sold me what he thought I wanted to buy. When I snorted it, I knew it was some kind of different. I heard that some guys at Hendrix had some Peyote buttons (the potent, hallucinogenic part of the Peyote cactus). These guys were from Hot Springs. They were a few years older than me, but I knew them from playing basketball together in the YMCA church league. They had a farm house somewhere out in the country, so my buddy Bob and I (both freshmen) went out there. They had the Peyote, so we bought some of the buttons and took them, being careful not to ingest the poisonous fuzz in the middle. It was bad enough anyway. Bob had a hallucination that he was being chased by a giant ham sandwich that was going to eat him (I'm not making this up). That was the last time he took hallucinogenic drugs. While we were at the house, I saw Burgess. He had to be the coolest guy at school. He had been a football star in high school and a street fighter. Then he became a hippie, grew his hair down his back and was a philosophy major, but he still wore his Hot Springs Trojan football letter jacket all the time. It was like he was so cool that he could wear something that was definitely not cool but because he wore it. He was saying "I don't care about cool," and that made it really cool.

My life continued on the same trajectory the rest of my freshman year. During the summer I moved into my family's lake house and worked with my Mom in the clothing store now that Dad was gone. Every night when I came home there were people waiting to party. I had the dope. I had the music. I was living the life I wanted. One of the more obscure bands I liked was a country rock outfit called New Riders of the Purple Sage. They sang the commentary to my lifestyle, "Dim lights, thick smoke and loud, loud music – it's the only life I've ever known." But that life got old quick. I saw people who wanted to be like me and I thought, "Why would anyone ever want to be like me?" God was at work among the purple haze. At eighteen, I had given up on life and was looking for an escape.

The Cross and the Switchblade

When I was in grade school, I was looking through the rotating book rack at Reader's Drug Store. It was across the street from my grade school and just a block from my house. Mr. Reader, the owner/pharmacist, was a short balding man with glasses. One time he had run for an elected office and didn't get many votes. My grandfather told him, "If I didn't have more friends than that, I'd carry a gun." As I spun the rack around past the comic books to the paperbacks, I was attracted to one with a reddish cover. It was "The Cross and the Switchblade" by David Wilkerson. I bought it and read the story of this country preacher who was called by God to New York City to minister to drug addicts, gang members and prostitutes. When I finished reading it, I thought, "That's the kind of thing God would do. He would take the worst people and change their lives."

In my summer of discontent, I heard that this same David Wilkerson was coming to Little Rock's Barton Coliseum. Barton was a big building on the grounds of the state fairgrounds. I had been there many times before for rock concerts. I once saw a guy attacked there in a random act of racial violence after a basketball tournament. That time, a black man had decided to attack the first white guy that walked by. He split his head open with a 2 x 4 and took off running. A friend and I heard the crack and tried to catch the assailant, but he was too fast. We returned to try to help the victim. The innocent medical student died a few days later and the composite drawing that my friend, Danny, and I provided helped capture and convict the criminal. My parents and pastor told me that I should never have gotten involved. I'd even been at Barton the weekend before David Wilkerson spoke to hear my favorite band the Allman Brothers Band with Dr. John "the Night Tripper" as the opening act. I knew something was wrong when hearing my favorite band live just didn't do it for me.

David, Burgess and Jesus

I decided to drive my Road Runner to Little Rock and hear David Wilkerson. Before I got out of town, Burgess pulled up in his truck beside me at a stoplight and said, "You want to go to Little Rock with me?" I said, "Yea." He parked his truck and got in my car and we headed off down the highway. Burgess had given his life to the Lord and had a deep, sincere faith, but I didn't know that. He said, "I'm going to hear David Wilkerson." I said, "That's where I'm going." That's where it started getting weird. He said, "I prayed that one of the guys on my job would come with me and no one wanted to go. I guess the Lord sent you to answer my prayer." I was thinking, "This guy talks to God and God listens." It freaked me out. I don't remember anything else about the hour ride, but I do know that when I got to the venue, I knew I was ready for a change. A guy named Dallas Holm sang some nice songs and then David preached a fiery sermon of challenge and commitment. I remember one point he made. "There's no such thing as a 50 percent Christian or an 80 percent Christian or a 99 percent Christian. If you follow Jesus, you have to give him everything." At the end of the service I prayed a prayer. It wasn't the one that Brother Wilkerson led. I made up my own that wasn't so eloquent, or faith filled. I prayed,

"God, I don't know if you're there. I don't know if you are who they say you are or can do what they say you can do. And I don't know why you would want my life, no one else does. But if you're there, and you can change my life, I give it to you, all of it."

I'm not sure I even said "Amen."

I am sure that God heard my prayer and changed my life. There were people going to the front of the auditorium, crying, deeply emotional, throwing their drugs and cigarettes onto the stage. I thought, "I can't go forward, Burgess is with me and that would just confuse everything." Then I looked up and Burgess was gone. I guess God was talking to him again. Then I reasoned that since I wasn't crying, no one would believe that I had really prayed. In the end, I didn't go to the front and Burgess returned and we walked back to the car. Traffic leaving the coliseum was bumper to bumper and I said, "We'll never get out of here." He said, "Let's pray about it." He prayed and immediately a car stopped in front of us and let us pull out. I was freaked out again, but knew I was on to something. I had been forgiven and set free. My addiction to drugs had been instantaneously, miraculously broken (I know it doesn't happen this way for everyone, but it did for me). The next morning, I gathered up all my drugs and drug paraphernalia and threw them as far as I could into the lake.

Burgess spent time with me that summer. We prayed together and read the Bible together. He helped me work through a David Wilkerson book for new Christians called "The Jesus Person Maturity Manual." I had become a Jesus Person, but most people called us

"Jesus Freaks." I knew that I had been delivered from sin, darkness, anger, bitterness, self-deception and so much more. I bought a Living Bible paraphrase of the scriptures, so I could understand better. I would read from the beginning of Matthew to the end of Revelation and then start over again. I couldn't read enough. I couldn't thank Jesus enough for what he had done for me. The people who used to buy drugs from me heard about how Jesus had changed my life. The people who used to come party at my house heard about how Jesus changed my life. The people who hung around the parking lots where I used to sell drugs heard it, too. A couple of guys moved in with me at different times the rest of that summer to hear more about Jesus and to stay away from temptation. I fell in love with Jesus more and more.

I went back to Hendrix College for my sophomore year. At the end of our freshman year, all the guys who were doing drugs agreed to live together, taking over two floors of one of the old dorms. When I went back to college, my roommate showed up with a huge bag of pills to sell. I would come back to my dorm room after class and guys would be there getting high. I just told them about Jesus. My roommate and I had lived together the year before, so he knew me really well. Someone asked him, "What's it like living with a Jesus Freak?" He replied, "I can tell you this, he's a lot nicer than he was before."

I found a group of sold-out Christians on campus and went to a prayer group each week in an old Episcopal Church in town. The group was led by some Charismatic Catholic women. I think some of them were nuns of some kind or another. Through their teaching and prayer, I experienced what Jesus said his Father had promised, being clothed with power from on high. I was filled with the Holy Spirit. I exulted in this new life. I was learning to walk in faith, learning to live in Christ, trusting him and obeying him in everything. I loved Jesus. I was so thankful for the ministry of the Holy Spirit in my life, and I knew God was Father, too. At least, I thought I knew this. Actually, I accepted the theological concept based on the biblical image of God as a Father.

Without being aware of it, I had carried the dynamic of my relationship with my father into my new Christian life. In the back of my mind the thought hung there, that God as Father had a high standard for my life. It was a standard that I felt I was failing to meet, and he was probably disappointed with me. Over the years, I developed a disciplined devotional life and worked faithfully in ministry. My focus was unswerving, and my efforts were exemplary, but somewhere deep inside I knew that whatever I did, it was not enough.

CHAPTER FOUR
A GOOD LOVE STORY

It was the perfect first date. We ate tasty fresh fish in a nice seaside restaurant in Virginia Beach. As the colors of the sunset were reflected on the ocean, we walked along the beach and talked. This was not superficial pass-the-time chatter. I found myself telling Nancy things that had been hidden deep within my soul. Things like hopes and regrets. I just felt comfortable with her, like she cared, like what I thought and felt really mattered to her. I put my arm around her shoulders because it felt right. I was never a touchy-huggy person. It was something my family just didn't do. Tonight, I did. I knew that it felt right. What I didn't know was that the Lord was speaking to her that he had created her to be there, next to me.

77 Pioneers

Getting to this point wasn't so easy. I had finished my degree from Hendrix College, earned a Master of Divinity degree from a seminary in California, then moved cross country to Virginia to be part of the 77-student first class of what is now Regent University. We came to be pioneers, graduate level students in Communications who would change the world. I can tell you my world was changed. It started in a chapel service. When I applied to attend the school (then called CBN University), they had projected launching two graduate schools, a School of Communications and a School of Divinity. In my application I proposed paying for part or all of my study in communications by working as a graduate assistant in the School of Divinity, since I had already earned a Master of Divinity degree. In the end, only the School of Communications was launched, but I still received financial aid, just not for teaching.

While the magnificent campus that exists today was still on the drawing board, we met in rented facilities in the Volvo Building on Greenbriar Parkway. The same space was used for library study tables and for chapel. The library did not have a huge collection at that time. The running joke was that the library was closed because the book had been checked out. It did, in fact, close for chapel. Each day for chapel service, the tables were put away and the chairs set up in rows. After chapel, the tables were put back up. That was my job. Maybe it didn't have the academic standing of a graduate assistant-ship, but it paid some of the bills, and the ability to set up chairs is a prerequisite for any ministry position.

Our chapel services were often spontaneous and highly inter-active. You could do that when there were only 77 students plus a handful of staff. We were all early adopters and we were making it up as we went along. The services were rich times of being led by the Holy Spirit with a strong sense of the Lord's presence and blessing. One of the early chapel services stands out in my mind. I remember hearing Nancy pray. I remember thinking, "That woman knows God." I also noticed that she was beautiful. I mean not just nice, O.K., better than average. I mean beautiful, the kind of beauty that lights up a room. What really stayed in my mind was the way she prayed. She was confident and bold, with a sense of a deep and intimate relationship with the Lord. That kind of intimacy and trust comes from a deep walk with God. It's a faith that has been tested through trials, hammered out by believing in God's goodness in the face of uncertainty.

We had a couple of classes together (that's no surprise, given the size of the student body where almost everyone is studying the same thing). One of them was Television Production taught by Bob Schihl. Bob had been a Vatican-trained Roman Catholic priest who had left the priesthood to marry a former nun. As Bob told the story, Nancy and I started sitting on opposite ends of the classroom, and as the term progressed we moved closer together until finally we sat next to each other. Our friendship began to grow as we took time to pray together and talk about Bible passages together. It was an easy, comfortable friendship that resulted in mutual encouragement and spiritual growth.

Raining on the Inside

I had suffered with depression all my life. I had never been to counseling or had a clinical diagnosis, but I knew how it felt. Sometimes things would just get dark. I would feel hopeless and alone. I knew the promises of Scripture and the life of Jesus, but still sometimes I would be overwhelmed. Many times, while in seminary I would pray, "Lord, I'm no use to you. Just take me home." I also knew the biblical promises for those who overcome, so I would try my best to be an overcomer. I had learned to ignore the darkness the best I could and just keep going.

One morning at CBNU, I felt the clouds of darkness move over my soul. As I had done so many times before, I did my best to ignore it and keep going. I was studying in the library when Nancy showed up, looked me in the eyes and demanded to know, "What's going on with you?" I gave some nondescript, generic answer like, "Nothing. I'm just studying." She wouldn't let it go. "Something's wrong with you. I've been praying and crying all morning. It feels like it's raining on the inside." I confessed to my on-and-off struggle with depression and that she had identified what it felt like, although I had never described it with those words. She started praying for me with fire and tears that the darkness would lift from my life. It did, at that moment. I was free, and I've never struggled with that kind of depression again. You can imagine that my thoughts about Nancy changed. She had prayed with faith and power, and I had been set free.

Over the days and weeks that followed, my appreciation for our friendship of spiritual encouragement grew. I was having romantic feelings for Nancy. I wanted more in our relationship. I also was afraid of what that might mean. It downright scared me silly. I had a couple of almost serious relationships in the years before I moved to Virginia. They started as friendships and moved from there to more than friendships, but in each one, what I initiated was not reciprocated. That's a nice way of saying I got burned, shot down and rejected (they were nice about it, mind you). I swore to myself that I'd stay away from the quicksand of relationships. You won't get sucked down if you don't go near them. I even wondered if I was some kind of psychological sicko who was attracted to women who would reject me. Yeah, I probably was, I thought. Now here I was on the doorstep. If I crossed this threshold, it was probably going to get ugly, go south, and be really, really painful. That's what my head said, but my heart was going somewhere else.

I'm not one for long phone conversations. For the life of me I can't understand how someone could talk on the phone for an hour and then turn around the next day and do it all over again. But that's just me. Except when I called Nancy for our first "date." She laughs now about how she knew why I called. I hemmed and hawed, talked about this and that. She was thinking, "O.K. when are you going to get to the point and ask me," and I just couldn't pull the trigger. Somehow, by the mercy of God, after a long, meandering conversation, I asked, and she accepted.

What Kind of Feelings?

That first date was magical. The next couple of weeks were a roller-coaster ride for Nancy. Unlike some (maybe most) of the other women at school, she really wasn't looking to get into a relationship with a guy. She had experienced more than her share of dating relationships that were pretty much all bad. We had both sworn off getting into a serious relationship. Over the next days, the Lord gave her prophetic direction that he was "in this." When she told me, I just couldn't believe that she would want to be with me. I'm too embarrassed to describe the exact conversation that took place. Let's just say that I responded like a dumb jerk.

Our first date was on a Friday night. A week later on a Saturday night, Nancy cooked a meal for me. She was living in a garage apartment in the home of the Vice President for Administration of CBNU. They let her use their kitchen and formal dining room. The family was out of the house. Convenient, huh? Nancy made lasagna. The placemats and napkins were a beige color with prints of maroon reptiles in a primitive sort of artistic style. The food was fantastic. For some guys, they're always comparing home-cooked food to the way Mama cooked. That was never a problem with me. My mother was a businesswoman and community activist, not a cook. I'm sure I would have continued to fall in love with Nancy without the delicious meal. The sparkle in her eyes was enough to dazzle me and capture my heart, but I won't lie to you. The delicious meal didn't hurt.

I was leading a weekly Bible study for CBNU students on Sunday nights in the home where Nancy was living. The students had become a tight-knit community, growing together in faith and relationships. The Bible study was an outflow of our sense of community and the study, discussions and prayer were life-giving. That Sunday night (a week and two days after our first date), I stayed to talk with Nancy after the other students had gone home. We sat on a couch in one of those not-very-often-used formal living rooms. I told Nancy that I had feelings for her (thinking that would get me a gold star). In a communication style that I now know, and at times even *appreciate*, Nancy probed. "What kind of feelings?" I dodged, "Deep feelings." Nancy probed again. "What kind of deep feelings?" I think I dodged and she probed a couple of more times until I said it, "I love you." She said, "I love you, too." I wasn't going to let her get away. If she would have me, I was going for it. I asked her to marry me and she accepted.

The next seven months of our engagement were not easy. Nancy was taking a course on "Conflict Resolution," and we used the insights from that class for all that they were worth. Like every other engaged couple, we both brought a lot of emotional baggage into the relationship. I was lousy at heart communication or expressing any kind of love or affirmation. I was pretty lousy at relationships in general, and my ineptitude was only amplified in one this deep. Nancy's mother had good reason to distrust men and she had taught Nancy and her sisters that it was a mistake to trust any man, especially one you were going to marry.

We kept trying to work through the misunderstandings, the uncertainties and the fears. We were determined that God had called us together and that he would guide us through the mess of our brokenness by his grace. We got advice along the way and most of it was bad. Nancy was told that when I did something stupid or insensitive (which happened often) that she should punish me by stonewalling, you know, refusing to communicate. The wife in the home where Nancy was living could tell that Nancy had been crying when she came home and would say, "What's wrong? This should be the happiest time of your life!" Well, it wasn't the happiest. It was one of the hardest. But we knew we were going for something genuine, from God, built on honesty and transparency. We knew we were laying a foundation for the long haul and if that meant digging through our emotional junk, we were going to dig until we hit bedrock. From bedrock to wedlock, I guess that's how it was with us.

Married

The wedding was beautiful. It was unusual, but beautiful. Nancy's sorority roommate from Indiana University was a concert harpist. Her music was inspired. They had formed a deep friendship when Nancy was a voice and theater major at IU. (Nancy's still one of the most talented people I know). Her maid of honor, Jocey, had led Nancy to the Lord during their time together at a summer stock production of the Stephen Foster Story in Kentucky. They then had filled Nancy's old green Ford with their meager possessions and moved out to LA to be part of a Christian theater group called The Hollywood Free Theater. My best man, Paul, a roommate in seminary, had flown in from Canada. My brother, Stueart, was one of my groomsmen. Nancy's Baptist family and my Methodist family were all there. The ceremony took place in a Charismatic Baptist Church in Louisville, Kentucky near Nancy's home. She and her mother had made the arrangements. The ceremony was conducted by our professor, friend and former Roman Catholic priest, Bob Schihl.

Like I said, it was unusual. Bob had stayed up all night in prayer and preparation for this holy moment. Nancy and I had written our own vows. I said mine and she got hers out between the sobs. Nancy looked stunning. After the reception, we flew off to Hilton Head, South Carolina for an idyllic honeymoon. We walked, rode bicycles, ate in restaurants, spent time alone and just enjoyed being together. Even though Hilton Head is known for its superior courses, I didn't play golf. It was a blessed beginning to our life together.

We bought a starter house in Virginia with part of the inheritance I had received from my father. I was going to school and working part-time for a CBN radio station. Later I worked for the Vice President of CBNU. Nancy had gotten a job at the 700 Club television program. She started as a researcher and writer, and continued to rise through the ranks as a reporter and on-air talent. When the producer saw her abilities and potential, he joked that he wanted to sign her to a lifetime contract. Life would have been much easier for Nancy if she had.

Hometown Bound

Instead, in late 1980 we moved back to Hot Springs, my hometown. We went from the growing prosperity of suburban Virginia Beach to the economically depressed South at a time when my hometown was at an all-time low. We moved into the lake house where the pipes froze and the lake had been drained for the winter. We looked out our picture window to see a huge mud hole surrounded by bare trees. The word "bleak" comes to mind. The house, well-suited for summer heat, never seemed to get warm.

I was working for a mean, argumentative radio station manager who had more enemies than friends. Someone cut down his broadcast tower and there were so many possible enemies no one was ever charged with the crime. Maybe the police thought he deserved it, too. He put up an 80-foot tower to replace the 400-foot one that was destroyed. The coverage area was reduced from three states to barely reaching the city limits, but he refused to lower the ad rates for the commercials I was trying to sell. I got paid $125 per week plus commission on my ad sales, only he kept changing the rules about what qualified for commission. I expected to assemble a group of investors, buy the station, create a flagship station with an innovative Christian format and then replicate the format in other markets until I took over the world for Jesus. (CBN was a place where big vision was part of the atmosphere). After about a year and a half, the old goat sold his station, but not to me. He did offer me first right of refusal, but I didn't have the $600,000 he wanted. At $125 per week it would have taken me some time to accumulate that kind of money (about 92 years if I didn't eat or buy clothes). The new owners offered me the job of general manager for that station and for a second station they already owned in town. I turned down their offer because I couldn't in good conscience promote the format of "raunchy country" as they called it.

When that door closed, I took a position as associate pastor of a growing church and continued to work in that position for the next 12 years. While I was trying to live out my dream of a life in ministry, Nancy was dying to many of her dreams. In some ways, it was like Joseph's 14 years of confinement, and it lasted about that long, too. She devoted her life to Jesus, to me and, in time, to our three wonderful daughters. Looking back with a long-term perspective on those years of raising a family, I'm sure I have some selective perception. Still, our family life was so rich and so full of life and vitality. Each of the girl's personalities was so varied. Each one is a unique gem reflecting its own beautiful light.

Nancy took every opportunity to bring joy and celebration into the home. A birthday celebration was good for a whole week; sometimes we'd stretch it into two weeks. Vacations usually meant travel to the beach to use a borrowed beach condo. The girls got to pick out their own favorite sugar-laden breakfast cereal. We ate our fill of seafood and walked on the beach every night. We watched the girls excel in school and in music. They played sports and took dance lessons. Nancy's years of sacrifice, giving up a television career, and pouring life and faith and vision into the girls' lives has born the fruit of confident, capable young women who excel in their chosen fields.

Life in ministry is difficult and demanding work with the added exasperation that the work is never finished. There are great highs of success and deep lows of betrayal and disappointment. My heart continually goes out to men and women in ministry. I know it can feel like a minefield, never knowing where the next explosion is coming from. It's my philosophy that even though we give our lives to Jesus and are used by him in ministry, the ministry can't be our lives. Our life in Jesus is not the same as life in ministry. Church work can become a monster that devours every resource of time, energy, and compassion. If this doesn't make sense to you, ask someone who grew up in a pastor's home to explain it.

I'm so thankful that I experienced the joy of being a Dad, and that I took time for kindergarten graduations, dance recitals, softball games and meals around the dining room table. Every night, Nancy prepared a meal and we ate as a family in our dining room (not the TV room). We talked about what kind of day the girls had, and just let them know that their lives, their feelings, their joys and struggles mattered. It was so much different from how I grew up. I really grew to appreciate the home and the life Nancy had created for our family. It was affirming, supportive and it was a safe place from the challenges of daily life. There was an atmosphere of healthy love.

After my twelve years as an associate pastor, Nancy and I began to travel and minister more internationally. Concurrent with some international ministry, we planted and led a church as co-pastors for eight years. Now we focus our efforts on international ministry through leadership development, educational programs, economic development, medical care and other forms of humanitarian aid. I'd like to tell you about the accomplishments of our daughters, but they would be appalled that I would write the long, long list of their accolades. Let's just say that Mom and Dad are really proud.

When I look at the wife and daughters that God has given me, I can only gaze in wonder at his grace, marveling at his goodness. Love has come into my life. It has been love incarnate, you know, love with skin on it.

CHAPTER FIVE
EMBRACED

There's a part of the story that I didn't write in the last chapter. It connects what has come before with what follows. I have trouble writing about it because I didn't see it. I guess everyone has a blind spot or maybe several. This is mine (or at least the biggest one I know of so far).

It has been very difficult for me to express love.

It was much more problematic for those living around me than for me. Nancy suffered because of this malady for years. While not excusing me, she was patient and tried to be understanding, but this thing in me didn't make life any easier for anyone. I know that, because people around me who love me told me. They tried to help me understand how important it was to others that I work to overcome this flaw, this handicap, this deficiency.

Expressing Love

Then came the intervention. Nancy, two of our daughters and I were in Tulsa where one of our girls lived at the time. We were in her apartment when the three of them began, in love, to open the wound. I don't remember the exact content or how the discussion started, but I do remember trying not to be defensive (my natural response) and trying to hear what they were saying. They knew my heart and my intentions, but they also knew I had an awful track record of translating those intentions into words. "Why is it so hard for you to express love? It's like you're closed up. Something is locked up inside." I tried to express my apologies to them one more time and tried to assure them that I had listened. I took it seriously.

I had been part of an accidental intervention once myself. My dad was drunk. I was 16 and was scheduled to play a basketball game in the YMCA church league (with the older guys who later had the farm house). I wanted to go alone. Dad wanted to take me. I didn't want to be embarrassed one more time. He was insistent that he was going to take me, and he was going to watch the game. We left the house together, but at the first stop sign I opened the car door and ran off into the night. I didn't have anywhere to go, so I just walked back home where he was waiting for me. He grounded me and told me I couldn't drive the car for a month or something like that. I think it really scared him to see what I would risk to keep from being out with him when he was drunk. The next morning he restored all my privileges. He was sober for three months after that, the longest stretch of sobriety I ever knew him to have.

After the Tulsa Intervention, I started to pray, really pray, doing what the Bible calls crying out to God in my distress. I wanted change. I wanted my wife and my daughters to know my love. If I could have changed myself, I would have done it long before this time. Only God could open my closed heart.

Toronto

Nancy and I had planted a church and served as pastors for seven years. My long-time friend, Rex had made plans to attend a four-week school on "Experiencing the Father's Love" at Toronto's Airport Christian Fellowship (TACF). Nancy suggested that I go, too. I said something like, "Four weeks is too long to be away from the church. I've got too much to do here." Then she threw down a trump card. "If you had a chance to train pastors in Africa for four weeks, would you do it?" Our hearts were growing more and more toward leadership training in developing nations. A couple of years earlier, I had spent several weeks in Africa training pastors. "Yea, I'd do that." At least I was honest. "But you wouldn't take the same time to care for your own soul?" She nailed me.

The signs of burnout were beginning to encroach on me. I was frayed around the edges, and it probably wasn't long before I would start to unravel. There is something biblical about that seventh-year sabbatical. "O.K., I'll pray about it." The more I prayed and thought, the more attracted I was to the idea of several weeks of inspired worship, reflection, extended prayer and biblical teaching. I also thought that I'd enjoy the time with Rex. We had served on a church staff together as associates and had maintained our friendship over the years. His wife, Clarice, had also served on that staff and was one of Nancy's best friends. This would be a good time to continue to strengthen our friendship. Over the years I had come to value the kind of God-given, heart relationship that I shared with Rex more and more.

The idea of "Experiencing the Father's Love" really didn't ring my bell, but I thought there would probably be some good content and helpful insights. One of the teachers was a guy from South Carolina named Jack Frost. No really, that was his name. (Jack Frost's ministry had been shaped by one of his mentors, Jack Winter. Truth is stranger than fiction). Rex and Clarice had been sending us some of his recorded messages for a couple of years. He had been a fishing boat captain in the Atlantic who had met the Lord and been called into the ministry through some dramatic events. He was a dynamic storyteller and that's always a plus for me. There were other teachers on the schedule who were unknown to me, but that was fine. I'm sure not stuck on big-name ministries. Too often fame is a function of being at the right place at the right time, catching a wave of cultural forces, and good marketing. I needed a heart invasion from the Almighty.

Rex picked me up at the Toronto Airport and we drove to the old warehouse building that had been converted, sort of, into the conference center. It was cold in Toronto in January and so was the building, but that didn't dampen the enthusiasm of the staff and the anticipation for the "Father Heart" school. Hoodies and heavy sweaters were everywhere. The people showing up for the school were a mongrel's mix. Students ranged from faithful grandmas and grandpas to representatives from the "what color will my hair be this month" tattoo and piercing crowd. They came from Europe, Asia, Latin America and the Middle East. One woman worked with underground believers in Muslim countries, another woman was just back from seven years on the mission field in China. One couple worked with Jewish evangelism in Israel and many were looking for "the next step" from God. And there was a pastor from Arkansas, too (me). Rex thought he had signed up for housing at the cold storage disguised as a conference site. There was no record of that. Thank God. So off we went, comparing prices at every hotel in the area to get the best deal on four week's lodging. The Best Western became our home away from home.

I soaked up the times of worship. Having been a musician, or the closest I could come to it, I appreciate technical skill. The worship leaders and bands were skilled, passionate and connected on a deep heart level. They were worshippers first and leaders second. Most were in training in TACF's worship school and were on loan to the conference. There was a rotation of worship leaders and players, and some of them were outstanding. There was a Scottish flavor to a lot of it due to the presence of some transplanted Scots, who are never ones to blend into the background. My heart softened as I got lost in the worship songs that were so meaningful to me. In times of difficulty, worship has been a lifeline for me. Time and time again, it has been a source of connection, strength, renewal and life. It has been a sacred place where I could pour my heart out to the Lord and receive faith and vision. As the school began and worship filled the hall, I went back to the sacred place of meeting Jesus in the swirl of diminished chords, backbeats and faith-filled lyrics.

There was a particular teaching session that stands out. It wasn't the first or second, but it was an evening session during the first week, early on in the school. I don't remember who the teacher was, but I'm convinced that they were following the leading of the Holy Spirit. Several scripture passages had figured prominently into the teaching. Central to everything at the "Father Heart" school was Jesus' story of the Father with two sons, what is usually labeled as the "Parable of the Prodigal Son."

On that night, the teacher invited anyone who struggled with a fear of failure to come forward for prayer. For me that was an easy one. I had felt the stinging accusation of failure repeatedly since childhood, and my Christian life was no different. The church hadn't grown fast enough, or the members weren't as deep in their spirituality as they should have been. I didn't pray enough, I didn't make enough money, and on and on it went. The threat of failure was never far away, like a vicious animal biting at my heels. I could never run fast enough or work hard enough to beat it.

Embraced

I walked to the front, closed my eyes, tried to open my heart and waited. The Holy Spirit came over me. I felt his sovereign presence. He revealed my heart to me. I saw what was in my own heart, and there were two parts to what I saw. On one hand, I saw how good God has been to me. Up to that point the doctrine of the goodness of God had been the most puzzling doctrine to me. Why would God be good to me? I had wrestled with this more than the doctrines of election or predestination. I knew they were a mystery. But the goodness of God was a conundrum. Here I was looking at God's goodness. I saw my marriage to Nancy and how she had been a blessing and an encouragement to my life. I saw our three wonderful daughters and how fortunate I was to be part of their lives. I saw how they all loved me. I saw the blessing of being called into ministry. God had taken me from a place of devastation and hopelessness and used me in ministry on four continents. God had been so good to me.

The other part of my heart was my fear of failure. He showed me how pervasive that fear had been in my life and ministry. He took me on a tour of my Christian life. I had made the top grades in school because I was afraid of failing. I had developed a disciplined devotional life because I was afraid of failing. I had studied scripture, mastered nuances of theology, worked hard at ministry, entered extended seasons of fasting, and challenged people to greater commitment and deeper discipleship all because of a fear of failing. I saw an all-pervasive motive for everything in my life. I had done all the right things for all the wrong reasons. The one thing that I wanted most – to get it right in serving God – I now saw as a place of failure. When I saw this, I said in my mind, "I've tried to hide my fear and now I've failed at the thing that was most important to me. I *am* a failure. It's just a matter of time before people around me realize that." At that moment I felt a deep, deep darkness envelop me.

It was a feeling of dread. It was the worst moment of my life. When I saw the motive of my heart, my worst fear had been realized.

Then something else happened. I felt God the Father run to me and wrap his arms of love around me, embracing me like the Father in Jesus' parable embraced his returning son. I felt his love pour into my soul. It was a healing love, and there seemed to be no end to it. I wept and wept and wept as I felt the Father's healing love pour into my soul over and over again. It seemed to fill my soul, overflow and then fill to overflow again. I was loved, not because of what I had done but because of who I was. I was his son. It was just so clear to me and so real. His love was more real than my fears and failures. My performance didn't matter. I was his beloved son.

The Holy Spirit then spoke to a big guy to physically embrace me. I felt these big arms envelop me, and I just kept crying and receiving, receiving and crying. Thirty years of labor and being heavy laden were pouring out of my eyes and onto this guy's shirt. I found out later he owned a pest control business in California. I think his name was Steve, but at that moment God was using him to be the Father's arms to a son who had come home. I can't describe the rest that came into my soul. There was a freedom and a security in the Father's love that I had never known.

On that January evening in that cold warehouse of a conference center, the Father's love transformed my life.

I continue to receive his healing love and cry "Abba" Father. I continue to feel his arms of love around me, embracing me, filling me, healing me, and loving me to life. Abba, Father, I love you. I have a Father now and he loves me.

For the next three and a half weeks, I continued to experience the Father's love both as an abiding sense of his presence and embrace, and – at times – an overwhelming, overshadowing of his power. I thought of Charles Finney's experience when he described being overcome by waves of love, so strong he thought that he would die. He cried to the Lord to lessen the power of love so that he could survive. I can't say that at any time I felt that I was near death because of the power of the Lord's presence (though it did cross my mind and I thought, "What a great way to go!"), but I can say I was repeatedly swept up into an overwhelming life that felt like love. I also drank in the teaching that re-examined the scriptures with a view toward grasping the revelation of God's love for us as a Father. The more I learned, the more I received this wonderful love. The more the love of the Father became an experiential reality; the more I wanted to study the scriptures to understand and grasp this overarching truth.

When I returned to preach in my home church, the first four weeks were times when the Holy Spirit brought deep healing and forgiveness as the congregation experienced outpourings of the Father's love. I continued to preach on the Father's love for months. I just couldn't stop!

CHAPTER SIX
A FATHER'S BLESSING

There was one subject that, whenever it came up, caused Dad and me to butt heads like a couple of bighorn rams. It came up a lot. It had to do with what I was going to do when I grew up. You can figure out by now that Dad had some ideas about this, and he was heavily invested in seeing that things worked out according to his plan. I had ideas, too, but they looked a lot different than his. He wanted me to enter some profession that provided a big paycheck. For some reason, I felt that God had called me into the ministry, and I couldn't be moved away from that.

What Do You Want to Do When You Grow Up?

I had grown up attending the First Methodist Church each Sunday with my family (my extended family on my Mother's side was all there, too). I admired the stained-glass windows and the dark ornate woodwork and had an idea that God was probably there. The sermons were about moral duty illustrated by nice stories, the best I remember. I also had a feeling that God was there when I floated through the beautifully dramatic canyons of the Buffalo River with my Explorer Post. The post Advisor was my Dad's good friend Pancho. Pancho had the pharmacy a few doors down from our clothing store. His real name was Jessie Calvin, but everyone called him Pancho, except my Dad, who called him Jessie Calvin. Everyone called my Dad by his nickname, Penny. Everyone except Pancho, who called him by his real name, Walter Alvin.

So I had this sense of God on special occasions, but I didn't have a heart knowledge of him or an experience of his love or forgiveness. Still I had a sense of calling to ministry. In Mrs. Freeman's fifth grade class, she asked us to draw a picture of what we wanted to be when we grew up. I drew a preacher behind a pulpit. It's nice that when a child is asked to draw something, they just do it. It's only later that we learn to say, "I don't know how to draw that." From then on, I was aware that I was called into ministry. I probably knew it before then, but that was the first time I remember expressing it in a concrete way. My grandmother, Nina Snow Stueart, was a praying woman. We have a needlepoint covered chair that belonged to her. I was told that this was her "prayer chair." She would kneel in front of this chair and pour out her heart to God. My grandmother was so proud that I was going to "make a preacher." But my Dad? Not so much.

We didn't butt heads much, but this was a tough one. Over and over, the conversation repeated itself as if Dad was going to wear me down and force me to capitulate if he hammered on it enough times. I was just as stubborn in my resistance. We stood at loggerheads until one weekend night at the lake house. I said earlier that my dad was not a mean drunk. He wasn't harsh or abusive, he just talked more. He talked about all kinds of things. Sometimes the two of us during fall or spring would spend the night together at the lake house, and he would get drunk and just talk. I think every son or daughter wants to know what's in their father's mind, you know, what are his thoughts and feelings, what's important, what's next? I didn't like my dad getting drunk, but I did like to know what was going on in his head, so these times together were kind of a mixed blessing for me. I liked the content but not the delivery system.

This certain night, "the subject" came up again. I was only about thirteen or fourteen, but I braced to stand my ground, unwilling to give an inch. We both knew where the conversation was going. At least I thought I did until he abruptly said, "I want to tell you why you have this desire to go into the ministry." Then the story unfolded.

A Father's Blessing

I've talked about my brother, Stueart, and how he didn't get the "win friends and influence people" concept as a child, or as a teen, or as an adult. After six years of wrangling with Stueart, my parents didn't want another boy. I guess they thought all boys were like him. They did, however want another child, and they tried to have one. Between Stueart and me my mother lost two children. When she became pregnant with me, she quit work as a beauty operator and sold her shop. That was quite a sacrifice. She had served as President of the Arkansas Cosmetology Association and continued to be active on a statewide level, as well as running a prosperous Beauty Salon with several employees. When I was born I wasn't a girl, but you've probably figured that out already.

Dad was disappointed.

I was born in Saint Joseph's Hospital, one run by the Sisters of Mercy Catholic Order. At the end of the hall on each floor was a large, almost life-size crucifix. That night at the lake house, in his altered state, my father told me that in his disappointment he walked to the end of the hall, looked at the crucifix and said, "This one is yours."

Seventeen years later in Saint Joseph's Hospital where I had begun my life, my father was coming to the end of his. I got the call from my mother, "Jim, you need to come to the hospital." I heard the urgency in her voice and picked up the undertones of fear. I came up the hospital stairs with my eyes quickly focusing on my father's heart monitor where I saw the flat line and I was gripped by the seriousness of the situation. I waited in anguish for something, not sure what I was waiting for. After what seemed like a couple of hours, my Dad's heartbeat had been restored and he was conscious. I know now that it was a miracle. Mom told me that I probably didn't want to see Dad. I said I did, so I went into his hospital room. He saw me and knew who I was. He may have spoken directly to me, but what I remember was an indirect comment he made. He said to the nurse attending him, "This is my son, Jimbo (the name he called me). He's going to be a preacher. He's not going to make a lot of money, but he's going to be happy." That's the last thing I remember my father saying. He spoke his blessing on my life in ministry. That night I slept at my Aunt and Uncle's house. The next morning someone told me that Dad was gone. The sadness started to settle in, but mixed with the heart-rending grief was a relief that I had received my father's blessing.

Jesus' Baptism

One of the core confessions of historic Christianity is that Jesus was fully human and fully divine. Yet when I think about Jesus, I focus on his divinity. I think about how different he is from me. He was God incarnate, having great knowledge and great power. In his gospel, John tells us that he was the only-begotten of the Father. That word is a translation of a Greek word that means unique or one-of-a-kind. He is the author of my salvation and the object of my worship, so it's hard for me to think about Jesus in his humanity or how he is like me rather than unlike me. Try to focus for a moment on Jesus in his humanity, rather than in his divinity. In his earthly ministry there were times when Jesus was hungry and tired. Surely, he was often disappointed by the low spiritual aptitude of his disciples. He knew sadness when he mourned the death of his friend John, the one friend who most understood who he was. Now go with Jesus, the man, to his baptism, looking at this event through the lens of his humanity.

Jesus understood that his baptism was the turning point of human history. Once he stepped into the Jordan River to be baptized by John, he could never go back. His obedience to the Father, to living in fulfillment of the law, his death through crucifixion followed by resurrection and ascension, would be the fulcrum on which human history rested. If he succeeded, humanity could be saved.

If he failed, all would be lost. The weight of the universe rested on his shoulders. Henri J.M. Nouwen has described Jesus' baptism as the "decisive moment of Jesus' life." (Here and Now, p. 190) When I first saw Nouwen's assessment I thought, "No, the cross was the decisive moment of Jesus' life." As I considered it more, I realized that Nouwen was right. The cross was the decisive moment in Jesus' life for me, but for him, it was his baptism.

We know that Jesus was tempted in every way, like we are, yet without sin. If he was tempted like us, could we say that there were questions in his mind as he looked at the Jordan River and at John, considering what was soon to transpire? Could he, like me, question that he was, in fact, the son of the Father? Could he, like me, question if he was really loved by God as a Father? Could he question if he was pleasing to the Father? I think those questions were somewhere in his thoughts. I think his identity with humanity went that deep.

As he came up out of the water after being baptized by John, a glorious drama unfolded. Divinity invaded humanity. Heaven was torn open and the Spirit descended upon Jesus in the form of a dove. A voice from heaven said, "You are my Son, whom I love; with you I am well pleased."

Identity

When Jesus heard his heavenly Father say, "You are my Son, whom I love; with you I am well pleased," his identity was settled. Jesus knew who he was. He knew he was loved and he knew his Father was pleased with him. The rest of Jesus' earthly ministry flowed from his identity as the beloved of the Father. This revelation and the confirmation it provided was the wellspring of Jesus' earthly life. His miracles and his teachings came out of the depth of relationship between Father and son. Jesus only did what he saw the Father doing and spoke only what he heard the Father saying. Theirs was a relationship of intimacy and power. Jesus could do what he did because he knew that he was the beloved of the Father and that the Father was pleased with him. What Jesus did flowed like living water from his knowledge of who he was. Who he was was determined by the one to whom he belonged.

Here's a question implicit in this glorious event. What was it Jesus had done to earn his Father's approval, his pleasure and his blessing? Why did the Father say, "I am well pleased with him?" The baptism was the beginning of Jesus' earthly ministry. Certainly, up to that point Jesus had perfectly obeyed the law or he could not have been the "lamb of God who takes away the sins of the world." Yet that doesn't seem to be the point here. The baptism was the threshold of Jesus' earthly ministry. It was the first act of the story, so it could be said that at this point Jesus had done nothing to earn the approval of his Father. That is the point. Jesus had done nothing to earn the Father's approval. The Father's approval was not for performance, but because of Jesus' identity.

The Father approved Jesus for who he was, his son, not for what he had done.

I was able to hold our first daughter soon after she was born. I wasn't prepared for the rush of emotions I felt in those first moments of her new life. A flood of love filled my heart and overflowed as I looked at this tiny girl, simply because she was my daughter. I loved her with an overwhelming love only because she was mine. It would have been silly to think that the source of my love was an expectation of performance. I didn't love her because one day she would clean my house or run errands for me or get a job and bring me money. I didn't love her because of what she could do. No, I loved her because of who she was. Her identity provoked my love, not her performance. I simply loved her because she was my daughter. Jesus was loved and the subject of the Father's approval simply because he was the son, not because of what he had done or would do. The identity as the "beloved of the Father" was fixed in Jesus' heart and was the foundation and source of the power of his ministry. What he did overflowed from the revelation of who he was.

Temptation

Jesus was not the only one who recognized the power of identity. Matthew's gospel (4:1-11) tells us that immediately after Jesus' baptism, he was led by the Spirit into the wilderness to be tempted by the devil. After forty days of fasting, Jesus was hungry, and the devil came to tempt him. The first question asked by the devil in his seductive conversation was, "If you are the Son of God, tell these stones to become bread." The goal of the devil was to trap the son of the Father by tempting him to prove his identity. He wanted Jesus to be seduced into the trap of proving his identity. If he was lured into proving his identity once, it would become an unending exercise, living his life try to prove who he was. (Maybe you can agree that the devil has not abandoned this devious technique). Jesus was not seduced into proving who he was. He knew who he was because his identity had been established at the baptism. There was no need for proof. It was settled. Jesus was the beloved of the Father and the object of the Father's favor. Because Jesus was settled in his identity, and because he knew the scriptures, he rebuked the devil.

A second time the devil tried to lure Jesus into the trap of proving his identity. This time, the temptation came cloaked in the guise of quoted scripture. "If you are the son of God," he said, "throw yourself down. For it is written, 'He will command his angels concerning you, and they will lift you up in their hands, so that you will not strike your foot against a stone.'" A second time Jesus refused to be baited into proving what he knew he already had. The temptation to do something to give evidence to Jesus' claim as the son of God was met once again with a refusal to capitulate to the devil's vapid challenge. Jesus rebuked the devil with scripture. Because of the Father's words at the baptism, Jesus was fixed in the knowledge of his identity as the beloved, favored son.

In the third temptation, the devil sought to engender worship in exchange for all the kingdoms of the world and their splendor. Jesus was offered a shortcut that didn't involve the cross. Without the cross, we could not know the relationship with the Father that Jesus knew. No deal. A third time Jesus rebuked the tempter with scripture and the tempter left. Luke's gospel tells us that Jesus "returned to Galilee in the power of the Spirit," and from there began his earthly ministry, bringing heaven to earth, the eternal to the temporal, as the Father's beloved son.

CHAPTER SEVEN
THE GREAT EXCHANGE

Were you gripped by the power of the Father's words to Jesus? Did you see the impact of the Father's love and approval in Jesus' life? Did you allow yourself to dream that you, too, could know the Father's love and approval?

Jesus prayed that you would. He went to the cross so that you could.

In Chapter 17 of his gospel, John records the High Priestly prayer of Jesus. This prayer, the longest of Jesus' recorded prayers, comes at a crucial time. He had completed his public ministry and was now looking onward to the cross. This was a turning point in his work. One part was complete, the other was ahead. At this critical juncture, Jesus utters this prayer for his disciples and for those to come. He pours out the petitions of his heart for them. In the last petition of this last prayer before the walk to the cross, he prays for you.

> *"Righteous Father, though the world does not know you,*
> *I know you, and they know that you have sent me. I have*
> *made you known to them, and will continue to make you*
> *known in order that the love you have for me may be in*
> *them and that I myself may be in them."*
> (John 17:25-26)

In this prayer, Jesus acknowledges to the Father "Righteous Father," that the disciples know that he was sent by the Father and that they know the son. The ultimate petition of this ultimate prayer is for the disciples (us) to know the Father's love in the same way that he knew the Father's love. He prays, "...that the love you have for me may be in them..."

That's why Jesus went to the cross.

Jesus lived his life in the experience of the Father's love and favor. He chose the cross so that those who believe in him could also know the Father's love and favor in the same way.

Yes, the cross took away our sin so we could be forgiven and so we could go to heaven to be with him eternally. But the cross did more than take away sin. It gave as well as taking away. It opened a glorious door of loving adoption, so that we could be the beloved sons and daughters of the Father, knowing his acceptance, approval and favor. We can live in the experience of his love, sharing his joy and delight through intimate and unhindered relationship.

In the Cross

In the cross, Jesus became who we were – separated from God by sin, alienated, without hope and on our own. He became who we were, so that we could become who he was – the beloved child of the Father. In his letters, Paul explains to the young churches this mystery of redemption. Often, he uses the language of the court-room to explain what has happened. Because of sin, we were under judgment, guilty and sentenced to death. Jesus became a sacrifice for us, dying in our place, taking our punishment upon himself and becoming our propitiation, to satisfy the judgment against us. In an imploring call to be reconciled to God, Paul succinctly states this wonderful mystery.

> *God made him who had no sin to be sin for us, so that in him we might become the righteousness of God.*
> *(2 Corinthians 5:21)*

It's a horrible and a glorious thing to see the cross and to see what Jesus endured to bring us back into relationship with the

Father. There was such unbearable physical suffering through the beatings, whippings and finally the torturous death on the cross. It was a death so gruesome and terrible that no Roman citizen could be sentenced to such a vile death. Beyond the physical torture, his heart was penetrated by the emotional pain of the rejection by those he came to save and the abandonment of those whom he loved. He was misunderstood by friend and foe. He silently accepted the false accusations and the unjust sentence.

This Cup

Still, there was a pain much greater than the physical pain or the emotional torment. It was Jesus' separation from the Father. In the garden of Gethsemane, Jesus prayed that "this cup" could pass from him. Jesus was referring to the cup of God's wrath that would be poured out in judgment. Jesus knew that if God's wrath in judgment were to be poured out on him, then the loving fellowship between Father and son would be, for the first time in all eternity, broken. Jesus would become sin and the Father could not look upon sin (Hab. 1:13). From all eternity the Father and son had been face to face (a more accurate translation of John 1:1[Morris, 76]), each gazing with love upon the face of the other. The moment on the cross that Jesus took the cup of wrath, the moment he became sin, the Father would turn away from him. Jesus would see the back of the Father where he had always seen his face. Jesus would take our rejection and our separation.

In the garden of Gethsemane, Jesus chose to take the cup and restore what was lost in the garden of Eden, and more. When Jesus cried on the cross the opening line of Psalm 22 (*Eloi, Eloi, lama sabachthani*) "My God, My God, why have you forsaken me?", he was declaring that he had taken sin on himself and experienced the rejection of the Father. He was also giving a key to those who understood the prophetic significance of Psalm 22. That psalm (written about a thousand years before the cross) and Isaiah 53 (written about seven hundred years before the cross) provide insight about what happened on the cross from a spiritual perspective. These ancient scriptures tell what happened as Jesus became sin for us that we could become the righteousness of God in him. He became who we were, slaves to sin, so that we could become who he was, the beloved of the Father.

Exchanged Blessing

There's a moving story in the Old Testament, found in Genesis 48 that illustrates an exchanged blessing in visual language. Jacob followed Abraham and Isaac (his grandfather and father) in receiving the blessing of the Lord and the promise of the covenant of blessing. Jacob's name was changed along the way to Israel, but that's another story and to keep things simple we'll stick to Jacob. Jacob's favorite son (out of twelve) was Joseph. Joseph's brothers were not so fond of him and sold him as a slave, telling old Dad that the favored son had been killed. Dad never thought he would see Joseph again, but God wrote the end of the story and it was a story of blessing and provision. That's another good story, but not this one.

This scene opens with Joseph bringing his sons to Jacob to be blessed by Jacob (their grandfather). Jacob was old and physically frail, having bad eyesight. With the news that Joseph and his sons were near, he rallied to greet them. In this dramatic moment Jacob repeated the blessing he had received (to be fruitful, increase, become a community and inherit the land) and announced that he was, in effect, adopting Joseph's sons, Ephraim and Manasseh.

In this wonderful moment, Jacob remembering the loss of his wife yet seeing Ephraim and Manasseh, calls them near, embraces them and kisses them. He tells Joseph that he never expected to see him again and now God has allowed him to see his (Joseph's) children.

Now is the time for the blessing. This is so important and it's vital that nothing goes wrong. There's a strict protocol that must be followed and Jacob can't see well, so Joseph must make sure that everything is as it should be. This is how it works. The greater blessing from Jacob comes from the right hand, and the greater blessing comes on the older son, so the older son, Manasseh, must be on Jacob's right. Conversely, the lesser blessing must come on the younger son, so Ephraim must be on Jacob's left. There's no room for mistakes here. Joseph knows this. Older son gets greater blessing on the right hand. Younger son gets lesser blessing on the left hand. The tension builds. Joseph checks and double checks that the sons are in their proper places. Older son, under the right hand and younger son under the left. Everything is set. Everything is as it should be.

Then something happens. It's something unthinkable, even tragic. Something unforeseen that changes everything. Jacob crosses his arms when he gives his blessing! They get the wrong blessings! The older gets the lesser blessing and the younger gets the greater. Joseph sees what's happening. It's like one of those horrible moments when everything goes into slow motion and the brain records every frame of the feared event. Joseph reached out, grabbing his father's arms to try to fix it. He implores his father, "No, my father, this one is the firstborn; put your right hand on his head." The scripture gives Jacob's response,

> But his father refused and said, "I know, my son, I know.
> He too will become a people, and he too will become
> great. Nevertheless, his younger brother will be greater
> than he, and his descendants will become a group of
> nations." He blessed them that day and said, "In your
> name will Israel pronounce this blessing:
> 'May God make you like Ephraim and Manasseh.' "
> So he put Ephraim ahead of Manasseh.
>
> (Gen. 48:19-20)

Jacob knew that he was giving Manasseh's blessing to Ephraim and Ephraim's to Manasseh and indicated that to Joseph by saying, "I know, my son, I know." It was no mistake. There was no confusion. The blessings were meant by Jacob to be exchanged. Represented in this historical drama of the faith is a picture of what transpired on the cross.

What belonged to us went on Jesus and what belonged to Jesus came upon us.

He became sin, he was rejected and he died. As Isaiah puts it (Isaiah 53:4-6):

> *Surely he took up our infirmities*
> *and carried our sorrows,*
> *yet we considered him stricken by God,*
> *smitten by him, and afflicted.*
>
> *But he was pierced for our transgressions,*
> *he was crushed for our iniquities;*
> *the punishment that brought us peace was*
> *upon him,*
> *and by his wounds we are healed.*
>
> *We all, like sheep, have gone astray,*
> *each of us has turned to his own way;*
> *and the LORD has laid on him*
> *the iniquity of us all.*

Through Jesus, we have become who he was, the beloved of the Father, pleasing to him. And the Father, who gave his son to suffering and sacrifice, says, "I know, my son, I know."

CHAPTER EIGHT
FATHER AND SON

When I realized that, through the cross, I could receive what Jesus experienced in his baptism, I started looking at his earthly life in a different way. His earthly life was a pattern of what it's like to live in the Father's love. His High Priestly prayer was that I would know the Father's love in the same way that he knew his Father's love. I realized that I had seen the earthly life of Jesus in a way that was, at best, incomplete and at worst, flat wrong.

I had seen the earthly life of Jesus as a prelude to the cross. Mark's gospel can roughly be divided in half with the first half telling the story of Jesus' first 33 years and the second half focusing on the cross. I'm thankful to the Holy Spirit working through Mark to show us the great importance of the cross and Jesus' substitutionary death. But there's more to the story. When I studied the centrality of Jesus' teaching about the kingdom of God, I gained an appreciation for the invasion of divine activity through his life. His works revealed the power of the kingdom; his teaching embodied the wisdom of the kingdom. But there's still more to the story.

When I experienced the embrace of the Father in my own life, I wanted to see what that looked like in Jesus' life living day to day, recorded in scripture. What would the text show me? What would the text say to me? How would the Holy Spirit teach me as I reengaged the scripture with new eyes to see and new ears to hear?

It's been my practice for more than three decades to read through the Bible each year. It's a discipline I've come to value and enjoy. I'm a creature of habit and this one is one of my best habits, for sure. Rather than the scripture reading becoming a rote performance I endure each day, my time of reading and reflecting is the first and often the best part of each day. When I read through the stories, the warnings or the words of worship, it's like visiting old friends. They are familiar yet fresh and alive.

But one year I (gasp!) broke my long-standing tradition and spent a year reading and re-reading the gospel of John. I read the 21 chapters of John over, and over again. I had one purpose in mind. I was watching the interaction between the Father and the son. I observed this dance of love that had existed in all eternity, had come into humanity, and was being expressed in a way that was intended to guide me into the same.

The Dance of Love

There are so many passages in John that speak of this dance. No one comes to the Father except through the son (14:6), and no one comes to Jesus unless the Father draws him (6:44). The Father loves the son and has placed all things into his hands (3:55). The Father glorifies the son and the son brings glory to the Father (8:54, 17:4-5).

Jesus encapsulates his whole existence, including his redemptive work in terms of the Father. Jesus explained this to the disciples by saying, "I came from the Father and entered the world; now I am leaving the world and going back to the Father." (16:28, see also 13:1, 14:12, 28; 16:10, 17).

There is an evident dependence of Jesus on his Father, which is portrayed as intimate and absolute. Jesus only does and says and imparts what he has heard and seen and received from the Father (3:11, 5:19, 8:26, 28, 40; 20:21). This dependence results in obedience, but not an obedience in response to slavish adherence to the law, but an obedience that is a doxological response to love. Jesus is loved by the Father and obeys the will of the Father in the dance of love.

One passage, John 5:19-20, seems to bring this out in especially clear relief.

Jesus gave them this answer: "I tell you the truth, the Son can do nothing by himself; he can do only what he sees his Father doing, because whatever the Father does the Son also does. For the Father loves the Son and shows him all he does. Yes, to your amazement he will show him even greater things than these.

Jesus says that he can do "nothing by himself." He is absolutely dependent on his Father. It's eye-opening to think that God-incarnate who healed the sick, calmed the storm, turned water to wine and raised Lazarus from the dead could do nothing apart from his Father. It's not that he *would* do nothing, but he *could* do nothing. He was unable, not just unwilling. The dependence was absolute. The key factor was love. "For the Father loves the Son."

To dig deeper into this passage, the wording in the Greek text (from which we get our various translations) may be surprising. The word that is translated love may be unexpected. Most people who have some familiarity with the New Testament, or have endured more than a few Sunday morning sermons, know that there are several Greek words that are translated into the English word "love." Each of these words has different shades of meaning. There's eros which refers to the physical expression of love. The English word erotic has its roots in this word. Another word is storge which refers to natural love, or one's own ability to love, which everyone knows comes to an end pretty quickly! Some have constructed a sort of hierarchy of love and next on the ladder is phileo. This one is often said to refer to fondness or liking, kindness or appreciation. It is sometimes described as "brotherly love." In America, the city of Philadelphia or "The City of Brotherly Love," gets its name from this word. At the top of the ladder is agapao (verb) or agape (noun). This is love that is from God. It is sacrificial, selfless and pure. A million preachers have defined agape as "God's kind of love."

With this Greek word study primer under your belt, which word do you think is the one found in John 5:20 describing the love of the Father for the Son? Most likely you would say, "agape." And you would be wrong. Take a step down the ladder to phileo and you would be right. The obvious question is, "Why would John record Jesus as saying that the Father's love for him was phileo rather than agapao?" It's because of how the Father and Son interacted in this dance of love. A biblical scholar can make a career out of digging into the nuances and shades of biblical languages. One paragraph just won't do, especially with a word as significant and powerful as "love." In digging a little deeper, the discovery can be made that the meaning of phileo can also include the sense of love that is demonstrated or felt. For Jesus, the love from his Father was not a concept of perfect good, as a philosopher might describe it. It was not an ideal to aspire to. It was an experience.

Jesus felt his Father's love.

The greatest need of humanity, at the core of our being, is to experience love, to be loved and to feel love. It was at this deepest place of existence and identity that Jesus knew the Father's love. He felt it. He lived daily in the experience of the Father's love.

Hugs and Kisses

When Jesus told the parable about the wayward son coming home and being embraced by his Father, he told the story in such a way that the hearers knew that the son felt the Father's love. He physically felt the embrace of arms around his body and kisses on his face. That's phileo. That's love that is demonstrated and love that is felt. Maybe Jesus came alive even more (if that's even possible) when he got to the place in the story that reminded him of his Father's demonstrated love and the love he felt as an abiding experience. This love was the impetus for his obedience to the Father. It was not a "this for that" obedience, like the law. This obedience was part of the dance of love between Father and Son that nourished Jesus in the core of his being and met his most profound need.

A Father with Two Sons

We call this parable, found in Luke 15:11-32, the Parable of the Prodigal Son. In the telling of the story, Jesus put the focus on the Father. He begins by saying, "There was a man who had two sons." I've been drawn deeper and deeper into this story because I want to learn how Jesus portrayed God as a Father. My teacher in this journey has been Professor Kenneth E. Bailey. One of Bailey's books was suggested to me by some dear friends, the Baileys, who also happened to be related to Kenneth. I approached the book as a favor to my friends and found a door into profound understanding of this story. In turn, I have been deeply impacted by his insights. Professor Bailey spent a lifetime living among modern Middle-eastern culture, learning about the culture that serves as the background of Jesus' teachings and helping Bible students rightly understand these teachings in their cultural context. Oh, yea, and he loved this parable. It was his favorite. Anything I would include here is only an insignificant footnote to his detailed scholarship and genuine grasp of this magnificent story. Please take the time to read his book. [*The Cross & the Prodigal: Luke 15 Through the Eyes of Middle Eastern Peasants* by Kenneth E. Bailey]

One of the keys to understanding the story is to understand who was listening when Jesus told it. He didn't write the story. He spoke it, and he had an audience who listened as he spoke. Any communicator worth her salt will tell you that to effectively deliver information, she must understand her audience. A talk to a biker gang would be approached differently from a devotional for a Girl Scout troop. Jesus was telling this story to two distinct groups. There were the sinners on one hand and the Pharisees and teachers of the law on the other. What put people on one side or the other was the law, or more exactly, the perception of their relation to the law. The sinners felt separated from God because of their failure to keep the law. The Pharisees and teachers felt justified because of their stringent adherence to the law.

When the people of Jesus' day thought about God, they understood him in three roles. God was Creator. He made everything that exists by his power. He was Law Giver. On Mount Sinai, God gave his law to Moses. It was a holy moment in the history of Israel and all that had come before and all that came after was seen in the light of the giving of the law. Finally, God was Judge. He would judge all people in relation to how they had kept the law. So Jesus' audience was made up of those condemned by their perceived failure to keep the law and those who were smug in their confidence that they had kept the law. To take it a step further, the Pharisees and lawyers felt they had been appointed by God to remind the sinners that they had not kept the law. A little guilt goes a long way.

When Jesus began telling the story of the outrageous actions of the younger son (actions that brought shame on the whole community, not just his family), it was clear who the sinner was. The sinners felt the weight of condemnation. The Pharisees swelled with a pompous, "I knew it," confidence when the boy landed hungry, penniless and friendless in the pig pen. Everyone thought they knew the end of the story. Then Jesus hummed a curve ball over the plate. The son concocts a scheme to work his Dad one more time. He really wasn't repentant, just conniving. (Check Professor Bailey's background on that one). Everyone knew that he would be beaten when he got back to the village, if not by his own family then by everyone else. A little street justice was waiting for this rascal, and he was deserving of every lick. But that's not what happened. The Father ran to the son before he could reach the village and get his comeuppance. The Father met the son with arms of love. The son tried to get on with his speech to negotiate terms, but the Father ignored it. He gave this boy the robe, the ring, the sandals and the feast. He was restored as a son. The older son was offended at this expression of love (and the prospect of losing more of his inheritance). He refused to come into the house and join the party. The Father went to the older son as he had gone to the younger. There's no indication that the older son responded to the invitation.

Jesus portrays God not as the Creator, nor the Law Giver, nor the Judge, but as a compassionate Father who forgives a son undeserving of forgiveness. Now go back to the crowd. Think about how this sounded to his audience. The sinners were thrilled. The law keepers were enraged. The determination of relationship with God as Father was not who was a good son and who was a bad son. It was not who had broken the rules and who had kept them. At the end of the day, one of the sons was at home in the Father's love and one of them wasn't. One son received the Father's embrace and one didn't. Jesus told this story to say, "This is who God is, he is Father, he is like a man who had two sons."

Are you at home in the Father's love?

My Son, Whom I Love

One more time, like Jesus at his baptism, it's easy to say, "Yea, that's great for Jesus, but…hello! I'm not Jesus. What about us fully-human-but-not-at-all-God people?" There's an answer for this and his name is the Apostle Paul. All right, Paul's not your average guy on the street, but he was a human. And he got this "demonstrated love" thing.

In Paul's writing to the emerging churches, he never used the term disciple. Instead, he chose to address those following his example in Christ as "my children" or "my dear children." He conveys his love as the primary dynamic in the relationship of spiritual leadership. In the first letter to the Thessalonians (2:6-8), he provides an inside look into how he approached ministry, giving insights into motivation and methodology:

We were not looking for praise from men, not from you or anyone else.

As apostles of Christ we could have been a burden to you, but we were gentle among you, like a mother caring for her little children. We loved you so much that we were delighted to share with you not only the gospel of God but our lives as well, because you had become so dear to us.

As Paul remembers his ministry in Thessalonica, he describes himself as gentle, comparing himself to a mother caring for children. A mother nurtures her children because she loves them, and that's Paul's point. Paul, the great theologian, the tireless church planter, the anointed one who worked miracles and endured persecution describes himself as a mother who nurtures her children out of love.

Is that a different description of Paul than the one in your thoughts? He's not finished. He talks about loving them so much and how dear they were to him. The teaching of content is there (the gospel of God), but Paul, the teacher, is motivated by deep love. Given the content, the theology wasn't enough for Paul. He was delighted to give his life as well. What he taught was imbedded in who he was, a spiritual Father, who gave his life for his children out of love.

Timothy

We are fortunate to be able to track the relationship Paul had with Timothy. There's one decisive moment in Paul's writings where the nature and depth of Paul's love for Timothy, like a Father for a son, shines through. Paul was addressing the church at Corinth. This was not a problem church, but a church with problems. It had lots of problems. Paul addresses those at Corinth as his "dear children" at a time when their behavior may have tempted Paul to disown them. He remained their Father in the gospel.

I am not writing this to shame you, but to warn you, as my dear children. Even though you have ten thousand guardians in Christ, you do not have many fathers, for in Christ Jesus I became your father through the gospel. Therefore I urge you to imitate me. For this reason I am sending to you Timothy, my son whom I love, who is faithful in the Lord. He will remind you of my way of life in Christ Jesus, which agrees with what I teach everywhere in every church.

(1 Tim. 4:14-17)

Paul acknowledges that there are problems and, as a Father, he is addressing these problems by sending Timothy as his representative. Timothy is faithful in the Lord and will remind the Corinthians of what Paul teaches. That's the plan. Those are the mechanics, yet there's a phrase in this passage that teaches volumes about how Paul did ministry. In the middle of the instructions he mentions Timothy's name. Did you see what happens after that? It's like Paul can't continue with the instructions. He interrupts himself to comment on his relationship with Timothy.

He says, "…my son whom I love."

Paul stops the parade, he interrupts the argument, and he pushes the pause button, to reflect on this deep relationship of the love of a Father for his son. Timothy is his spiritual son or his son in the gospel but that passionate, holy relationship can't be sublimated by the task at hand. When Paul says Timothy's name, he has to interject, "…my son whom I love."

You and I were created to be loved and that love is not an ideal or a perfect concept. That love is an experience that we feel in the depth of our being. We were created to be loved by the One who created us and by those who have the Creator's life and love within. The example for that demonstrated love is in the dynamic relationship of Jesus and his Father in the New Testament and, most clearly, in the Gospel of John.

Read it again with new eyes and ears. Expect to feel the Father's love.

CHAPTER NINE
NO LONGER ORPHANS

It was at a training session similar to many I've conducted for church leaders in Asia. We had been "smuggled" into the meeting hall at 5 a.m. because a policeman watches the building for suspicious activity from 9 a.m. to 5 p.m. each day. Gathered together was a group of about 60 youth leaders from across Vietnam. They were in a room where 40 would have been crowded. There were no chairs. They stood to sing and pray, with great exuberance and expression, and sat on the floor during the teaching. It's hard to communicate the explosive joy that was packed in that small room and hard to fathom the presence of joy knowing that these young women and men constantly face the threat of persecution.

I would be teaching that morning on the Father's love, but I felt that I should start with an approach that I had never used before. I began with the scripture recorded in John 14:18, "I will not leave you as orphans; I will come again to you." I taught about the Garden of Eden and how we became separated and orphaned from our Father. From that time, he has been at work to get his family back. Now through Jesus, we can be adopted into the Father's family. We are no longer orphans. We have been adopted by the Father.

I've had a lot of translators over the years. Some of them have been good and some of them, well, have given me the opportunity to grow in grace and patience. And repetition. This time, my Vietnamese translator was a young man who was one of the best. The more I preached, the more involved and excited he became. The more engaged he became, the more I preached with confidence and intensity. The preaching overflowed into a time of prayer together where we experienced the Father's love deep in our souls.

After our time of ministry, I asked Minh to tell me about his life. Then I understood the passion in his heart about the adoption of orphans. Minh's father was an officer in the South Vietnamese Army who was sent to a reeducation camp after the fall of South Vietnam to the communist North in 1975. Minh's father was not married to his mother. He was married to another woman and had five mistresses, one of whom was Minh's mother, so even after his father returned from the camp, he was not welcome in his father's home. Although his mother and father were both living, he grew up like an orphan, living wherever he could find someone who would take him in. Sometimes he lived with a grandparent, sometimes with an aunt or uncle but never truly having a home. As a young teenager, Minh left what family he had in the countryside and moved to Ho Chi Minh City, formerly Saigon, to find work and try to make a life for himself. He lived on the streets until he could find work.

What he found was the most difficult kind of construction work. He spent hours breaking rocks to earn enough money to survive. With his intelligence and determination, he was able to feed himself and live a meager existence in the city. Often, he would see children on the streets. He would ask, "Why aren't you in school?" They would reply, "We don't have money to pay the school fees." He would ask, "Have you eaten today?" They would usually say, "No." Minh would then spend any money he had to buy bread to give to the children from the streets.

As Minh worked diligently to improve his condition, he never forgot about the orphans. When I met him, he and his wife had nine adopted children. He also provided support for more orphans in his home area. His dream was to start an orphanage, but because the government knew he was a Christian, they wouldn't allow him to perform any social services. The only way he could care for orphans was to legally adopt them into his family, and that's what he had done, nine times.

I then understood why I felt that I should begin with the scripture that "I will not leave you as orphans." And I understood why Minh was so passionate as we worked through the message about the wonderful gift of adoption and receiving God's love as a Father. When I shared this story with a Philippine ministry associate, who had set up the training in Vietnam, he helped me understand how this message had touched a deep need. He said, "In the Vietnam War, America lost their sons, but Vietnam lost their fathers. Vietnam is a nation of orphans." For me, as an American from the last generation, to speak to Vietnamese young people about being adopted by the Father had an impact far beyond what I could imagine. In the Vietnam War, or as they call it, The American War, America lost 57,000 young men. The death toll in Vietnam was 3 million. The Holy Spirit was working in a way that was beyond my grasp to bring redemption and healing through the revelation of his love as a Father.

Since that first long day of ministry together (teaching and preaching from 5 a.m. to 11 p.m.), Minh and I have continued to grow in our love and respect for each other. We've collaborated on many ministry projects and together are thankful for our Father's love and the spirit of adoption.

Abba, Father

In his writings, the Apostle Paul is moved by the Holy Spirit to provide insight into this wonderful adoption into the Father's family. Paul's letter to the Ephesians has been called the "Alps of the New Testament" because of the heights of theological perspective it provides. After the initial greeting, Paul launches into an out-flowing of gratitude for our blessings in Christ and at the top of the list is being adopted.

Praise be to the God and Father of our Lord Jesus Christ, who has blessed us in the heavenly realms with every spiritual blessing in Christ. For he chose us in him before the creation of the world to be holy and blameless in his sight. In love he predestined us to be adopted as his sons through Jesus Christ, in accordance with his pleasure and will— to the praise of his glorious grace, which he has freely given us in the One he loves. (Ephesians 1:3-6)

Before the world was created, our loving Father chose us to be adopted into his family, where we experience all the security, affirmation and provision we need. Whew! That kind of love and kindness, given to us before we could have done anything good, is too deep to understand. We can only stand in awe or bow in humble worship in view of such gracious love.

When the reference is made to "sons," this includes both men and women. At the time when the New Testament was written, the inheritance of the Father went to the son or sons. Both men and women are included in the inheritance of the Father, so both are included here. Maybe there's a flip side when the church is referred to as the "bride of Christ." Both men and women are part of the bride. So, in the New Testament writings, women may be sons and men may be a bride. These are cultural analogies that help us tap into amazing spiritual realities that are beyond our comprehension.

Paul teaches us in Galatians (4:1-7) which was sort of a first draft, and again in the more fully developed Romans (8:12-17), that in Christ, we have been delivered from a spirit of fear, which brings bondage, into the spirit of adoption or sonship. The Holy Spirit witnesses to our spirit that we are God's children. The witness of this adoption is a cry of "Abba, Father." This cry comes from deep within our being, from the deepest part. It's a cry of deepest love and absolute trust. To cry, "Abba," is a declaration of intimacy reflecting access to the Father's heart.

In New Testament times, "Abba" was an intimate form of address used in the homes of Aramaic-speaking families. You can imagine that I've shared these truths in dozens of different cultures and languages. In every one so far, there are two names for Father.

One is more formal, like "Father." The other is more intimate, like "Daddy" in English. It's always endearing to me when my thirty-something-year-old Chinese spiritual "son," who is well educated and a successful businessman, calls me "Daddy" and gives me a hug. "Abba" carries with it the sense of naïve trust, complete dependence, and intimate relationship that brings rest and security. This is our heart cry when we know the Father's love.

It makes sense, doesn't it, that we cry from the depths of our beings for rest and security. We try to find a rest for our souls and security from trouble in a thousand different venues, but it's only found in one place. It's no wonder that our hearts cry "Abba, Daddy, Father" when we experience satisfaction for the longings of our hearts. It's the deepest satisfaction for the deepest longing. There's a soul rest and a profound satisfaction in knowing that we've been chosen before the creation of the world and we've been adopted in love. We know who we are because we know that we're children who are loved with a perfect love by our Abba.

Roman Adoptions

When Paul writes of adoption, in his mind is the example of the formal adoption of a son by a Roman citizen. It was very important for a Roman citizen to have a son to carry on the family name or *pater familias* and to receive the family inheritance. If a man and his wife could not conceive a child, adoption was an option to fill the void. The first place to look for a candidate for adoption as a son was in one's own household. The son of slaves could be adopted. As painful as it would be for slave parents to give up their son, they knew it would be the best path for the son for the rest of his life. Slaves were held in bondage, living their lives in servitude generation after generation often because of a debt that could never be fully repaid.

When a slave son was adopted into the master's family, several things happened. And they were all good. First, their son takes on a new name, the family name or *pater familias*, and with the name comes an inheritance of the master's estate. Everything that the master owned would now belong to the adopted son. Second, the son would become a free man and third; all the son's previous debts would be cancelled. By now you can see the parallel of adoption of sons to the blessings of those who are in Christ. We have received a new name (or identity), a new inheritance and all debts have been cancelled. This transition is not earned but declared done by the one who has authority to do so.

There was an official ceremony called the *Adoptio Sensu Strictu* where the adoption took place. It was performed before a Roman magistrate. The adoptive free parents and the natural slave parents would stand facing the magistrate with the boy in between the two sets of parents. Three times the natural father sells the boy to the adoptive father and each time the magistrate observes the boy moving from the old parents to the new ones. These movements represent the change of fatherly authority or *patria potestas*. After the third transaction the magistrate declares, "This boy is now adopted as your son." Money changes hands and the boy is now the new father's son and heir. He is free. His debts are cancelled. He has a new family, an inheritance and a future. [Stibbe 29-30]

This was the symbolism in Paul's mind as he writes these words in Colossians 1:13, "For he has rescued us from the dominion of darkness and brought us into the kingdom of the Son he loves." We have been rescued from the bondage of slavery to fear, into a relationship of sonship, crying, "Abba, Father."

Rejection and Abandonment

The testimony of the New Testament is that the love of Abba, Father meets the deepest needs of our souls. Included in that bundle of blessing is the conquest of fear. This is the fear that leads to bondage or slavery that Paul speaks of in contrast to the adoption of sons. It seems to me that our most profound fears are the twin fears of rejection and abandonment. My drive to perform to my father's expectations was an expression of my fear of rejection. I wanted my Dad's approval. I didn't want him to reject me. The fear of rejection pushed me to try to earn the security of his acceptance. But there was no rest in that perpetual effort. I was only as "good" as my last success, whatever it might be – a good grade in school, an award in Boy Scouts or stacking shirt boxes properly in the clothing store. Each day brought an opportunity to fail, to fall short of expectations, and ultimately to be rejected on some level. A shepherd leads his flock, but a butcher drives his. Fear is a butcher that drives mercilessly until death comes.

The great evangelist Billy Graham understood the ruthless, unfulfilled drive of fear. Often when making the appeal for salvation in Christ, he would say something like, "You feel lonely and alienated. Come now and receive Jesus as your Savior." Do you remember the other part of the invitation? "The busses will wait; you come now." (Here's some advice: Never let a waiting bus deprive you of eternal salvation). No one really wants to live alone and certainly no one wants to die alone, yet Graham knew that alienation is a soul disease of this generation. It is both a fear and a reality.

Back in my hippie days, I went with two friends to a concert. As usual, we were in an altered state and my buddies decided to play a trick on me. Tricks, or "head trips" as we called them, were easy to pull on people with non-functioning brains. As we went into the concert hall (this one had open seating), they would point to some free seats and say, "Let's sit there." I would take off, going down the row to get halfway to the seats and realize that my buddies had taken off in another direction. I found them again and they played the same trick on me a second time, directing me to go down a row of seats and then abandoning me. Yea, it was another sign of low brain function. When I looked around and realized they were gone, a clear voice pierced the mental fog. It said, "You're alone. You were born alone, and you'll die alone. You're alone." Like a robot I mechanically repeated in my mind the condemning words I had just heard. "I'm alone. I was born alone, and I'll die alone." I've often thought about that lie of the devil, which I embraced at the time. I think about the blessings of relationships in family, coworkers, and spiritual sons and daughters that the Lord has given me. I think about the intimacy and satisfaction I know in my Father's love and I know that I'm not alone. Even if no one is around me when I die, I won't die alone. I am my Father's child and he is my Abba, Father.

I don't know how the fears of rejection or abandonment have made their place in your life, but I'm guessing that somehow, they have come to dwell in your soul. You know the torment of the fear of being rejected or abandoned. It usually enters our souls through some deeply hurtful event. There was something that happened that made you feel vulnerable or violated. You were wounded in your soul, and that wounding event became wet cement where the devil embedded one of his lies. He took away your sense of rest. You were no longer secure. Fear entered, and the torment began. For some the event may be more traumatic than for others; for some the pain more pervasive than for others. But living in a fallen world, the experience of soul-wounding events, and the accompanying lies, is inescapable.

The Father's love is a healing love.

Where there has been fear and slavery, there can be freedom and a restoration of rest. Where there has been the alienation produced by fear of wounds, there can be the embrace of the Father's arms. Where the lies of the enemy have brought destruction, the truth of who we are and whose we are can restore us into the vibrant, creative, fruitful men and women the Father created us to be.

When I was maybe 7 or 8 years old my mom took me to summer camp. I was big on summer camps and went to several of them.

I guess I went to camps because my parents were looking for something for me to do during the summers. Anyway, we loaded up the station wagon with my stuff and took off. Our car at that time was a 1959 Chevrolet station wagon. It was quite stylish with two shades of green paint and lots of chrome. In the late 50s, chrome was king. What distinguished that car were the tail lights. They seemed to be designed by someone who also designed "cat eye" glasses – the ones that swept up and out to a dramatic point. Imagine some of those glasses filled with red lights and outlined with chrome and you've got a picture of those distinctive station wagon tail lights. They were surpassed in dramatic design only by the Cadillac of the same year. That thing had fins like a land shark.

Mom drove me to Camp Yorktown Bay. It was in a bay of the lake and named after Yorktown, Virginia where George Washington won a decisive victory over the British. We registered, found my cabin, and put my stuff on a bunk. We said "goodbye," and she drove away up the hill and off the property. The camp was O.K. at first. I swam, shot archery and made crafts with the rest of the kids. I could tell the counselors were not really committed to the task of enriching children's lives. It was more like they were just killing time and getting a small paycheck until they went back to college. The kids in my cabin ended up running up a mountain road. Lots of times. Like every time we bugged the counselor. Just about everything bugged him. I wasn't having much fun, and I was getting more homesick by the day.

Then I had "the dream." I dreamed that the time had come for camp to be over. Mom came to get me but instead of stopping to pick me up, I saw her circle through the camp and then drive up and over the hill. I ran after her, trying in vain to catch up with the car, feeling the dread that I couldn't, and felt the exhaustion of energy spent for nothing. I stared at those cat-eye tail lights until they disappeared out of sight. In my dream — and I remember the exact words — in desperation I screamed, "Doesn't anybody care about me anymore?" Only it wasn't just in my dream. I screamed so loud that I woke myself up. I was glad to see that I hadn't roused anyone else but sad to realize I was still at camp and the week wasn't over. Mom did come get me and, unlike the dream, she stopped in front of my cabin, loaded my stuff and we drove home.

For many, abandonment is not a dream but a nightmare with the pain multiplied by its reality. Corrie ten Boom survived the horrors of a Nazi prison camp and witnessed the death of her sister amidst the atrocities there. She knew a deep soul pain. Her exhortation was that "There is no pit so deep, that God's love is not deeper still." We long for love because we were created to live in love. The fears of rejection and abandonment are scars left from the fall, made deeper and more painful by the repercussions of living in a fallen world. Still, the Father's love is deeper still.

The List

There's a story of a young woman who was engaged to be married. As the time for the wedding grew near, she imagined how wonderful her life would be. All her life she had imagined that marriage would be the fulfillment of all her dreams. She would be loved, appreciated, affirmed and fulfilled. Soon after the wedding, her new husband began to change. He no longer said nice things to her, or spoke of her beauty, or his love for her. He became more demanding and more violent in his actions when his demands were not met. Each day before he left for work, he presented her with a list of tasks. When he came home, he looked over the list. Her efforts to accomplish the tasks on the lists never satisfied his expectations. He would tell her what a disappointment she was, how she couldn't do anything right. Why did he ever marry her? She was a failure as a wife and on and on it went. Each day he gave her the list. Each day she worked as hard as she could, yet each day her efforts were met by a tirade of insults and condemnations. She tried to tell herself that it didn't really matter, but it did. Day after day the insults she heard and the isolation she felt were wearing away her soul. No matter how she tried, she couldn't placate him; she couldn't satisfy him and in time she couldn't stand him. She was a prisoner in her own home, tormented by fear and condemnation. And then suddenly, he died. Maybe the anger got to his heart. She didn't know the cause and didn't care. The nightmare was over.

It took a long time to get her life back. The scars of abuse had inflicted deep wounds. But little by little, she began to think differently about herself. "I'm not such a bad person. I can do things right." She started to listen to music again. She took long walks through the woods. She read books about adventurous women and dreamed of a better life. Then she met another man. The hope began to grow that marriage could be a good thing. She dreamed once again about being loved, valued and affirmed.

A second time, she was married. This time was different. Her husband told her how wonderful she was, how blessed he was to have a wife like her. They took walks together and ate dinners by candlelight that she lovingly prepared. When she cleaned the house or ironed the clothes, she would sing and dance from one room to the next, full of joy and wonder at the life she was living. One day she was cleaning out an old chest of drawers when her eyes fell on a piece of paper shoved back into a corner. She knew immediately what it was. It was one of the old lists from her first husband. Dare she touch it? Even open it? She didn't want to. She wanted to close the drawer and never think of it again, but she couldn't. With trembling hands, she touched it, pulling it out of its dark hiding place. As she did, the feelings of fear and condemnation all flooded back into her soul. She remembered the darkness and torment of her former life, but she had to see what was on the list. As she opened it and read it, she realized that all the tasks on the list were things she was doing now for her new husband. What she had once done out of fear of condemnation, she was now doing out of a response of love, as a gift to the one who loved her.

I think this is what the Apostle Paul was getting at when he writes, "For you did not receive a spirit that makes you a slave again to fear, but you received the Spirit of sonship. And by him we cry, 'Abba, Father.'" (Romans 8:15)

On the cross Jesus took the fear, condemnation and punishment of our failures. Instead of rejection, abandonment or isolation, we have been adopted into the Father's family. We have a place of rest and security in this intimate relationship with Abba. He took the initiative to draw us near, to wrap his arms around us and tell us that we are each his child, he loves us and he is pleased with us.

CHAPTER TEN
FORGIVING FATHER

By now, you've probably seen that, for me, experiencing the Father's love has touched me deeply and transformed me profoundly. I've experienced his love in a deep place that I didn't even know existed. Deep calls unto deep, as the psalmist says. There's a dimension to this experience that I could describe as mystical. I can understand the Father's love to a point. I can study the theology, read the scriptures and analyze Jesus' teaching – and I certainly enjoy that. Yet, the experience of the Father's love goes places where rational analysis and categorization cannot go. C.S. Lewis used the term *supra rational* to describe the reality of spiritual life that lies outside of the scope of rational thought.

After I experienced the Father's love in Toronto, the Holy Spirit led me to see things differently. In his ministry as teacher, he taught me more about the Father, about Jesus and about me. One of those lessons was essential to my continued spiritual formation and growth, but it came as a shock. I didn't see it coming. In a time of prayer and reflection, I was thinking about my father. In my mind, I saw his face. The look on his face was one I had seen hundreds of times but had chosen to forget. It was the look in his eyes that caught me. They were glazed and dull, the way they looked when he was drunk.

Why would I envision my Dad like this when I could have pictured him in other ways that were more favorable? Was the Holy Spirit at work? Was he showing me something and leading me to face something that I didn't want to see? I felt that he was, so I tried to follow down the path he was taking me. Did I need to forgive my father? Several times on my journey of spiritual growth, I had intentionally forgiven anyone who I thought had wronged me. I remember speaking words of forgiveness to my father, or maybe to the memory of my father more than once.

Even so, at that moment I sensed that I had buried wounds I felt from my father's drunkenness under a layer of denial. In trying to obey the leading of the Holy Spirit, I owned up to my offense toward my father. In my mind, his decision to abuse alcohol resulted in actions that disappointed and embarrassed me. I again went through the process of speaking words of forgiveness. I brought into my mind the compassionate thoughts that he did the best he could. His father was an alcoholic and probably his grandfather. He didn't know about the power of the Holy Spirit to set him free from his addiction. I said, "Dad, I love you. I forgive you."

Forgive and Receive

While praying with people from a wide range of backgrounds and cultures, I've come to see that forgiving our earthly fathers is an essential part of receiving love from our heavenly Father. What was your father like when you were growing up? How would you describe your father? The responses to these probing questions cover the spectrum of human experiences. They range from the best in human nature to the worst, from the most inspirational stories of love and sacrifice to the most horrendous examples of tragic abuse. For some, their relationship with their father was imbued with hope fulfilled. They were lovingly affirmed and carefully protected. Accomplishments were met with reward, failures without rejection. People with fathers like that are blessed, but sadly, fathers like that are rare.

For others, their fathers were absent, removed or just unengaged. They just didn't seem to be part of the picture emotionally, if not physically. A hole is in the soul, and there's a deep longing for the affirmation that never came. Dad wasn't there at ball games or music recitals or awards banquets. Seeds were planted in the soil of insecurity that later germinated and grew into fears of abandonment.

I have a friend who grew up with a brother and a sister. His parents' contentious marriage often erupted in verbal arguments with threats of divorce being hurled back and forth. The three kids often heard the arguments at night, listening intently while they cowered in the protection of their beds. One night the parents went on a tear about who would get what in the impending divorce (which never happened). They came to custody of the children. Dad wanted his brother. Mom wanted his sister. He waited in gripped anticipation to hear who wanted him, but his name was never spoken. No one wanted him; at least, that's what he heard. And, as he tells it, he's spent the rest of his life, through four marriages, trying to prove that he's worth being loved.

Some people are like me and had a father who was demanding. Love seemed to be conditional and the fear of failing was ever present. At one time I thought this was a generational thing. The fathers of his generation just didn't express affirmation. They had been through World War II, and the expectation was for sons (especially) to "man up." They didn't acknowledge emotions and feelings. They just did what needed to be done. They were task-oriented, valuing discipline and hard work. But that's just not true. Or maybe it was true of them but not exclusive to them. I see men like my Dad who struggle with showing love and communicating affirmation all over the world. The effect on their sons and daughters is the same.

Then there is the negative extreme. It's the heartbreaking end of the spectrum where what should have been one of the better parts in life became the worst. A father who should have been protective took advantage of a child's vulnerability. The father became the source of unspeakable torment through abuse. The way out of an abusive childhood includes passing through the door of forgiveness. I've seen this, and it has been an amazing testimony to the power of God's grace. I've had the honor of watching men and women who were brutalized through abuse speak words of forgiveness to the men who perpetrated these horrible things. I've seen the amazing transformation as these men and women are released from the prison of resentment and fear because they did the one thing they thought they could never do: forgive their father. I've seen them change as forgiveness severs the tethers that held them captive to terrible memories. They didn't feel forgiveness but chose in faith to extend to their fathers a gift that was undeserved. By moving into the plan of God for freedom, they found the release that never came through fight or flight. The freedom came through forgiveness, and forgiveness came through the supernatural grace of God.

For the follower of Jesus, forgiveness is a non-negotiable. The requirement to forgive is absolute, no exceptions and no exclusions. It's not like a food item in a cafeteria line where you can choose what appeals to you and pass by what doesn't. (Matthew 6:12 and Luke 11:4, Luke 17:4, Ephesians 4:32, Colossians 3:13).

On the Other Side

Forgiveness is like a door that swings both ways, at least for me. The Holy Spirit led me to greater healing and restoration through the forgiveness of my father. He then led me to reflect on my own fatherhood. Nancy and I have these three wonderful daughters, and I am so thankful for who they are. Many times, as I watched them grow up I thanked the Lord that, through his grace and power, they didn't have to grow up with an alcoholic father. My Dad was gone by the time I graduated from college. He drank and smoked himself into the grave soon after my high school graduation. I thought about that as I proudly attended each of my daughters' graduations. They each graduated near the top of their classes, winning awards and recognition for excellence in their chosen specialty. They are high achievers and have been since starting kindergarten. There have been only a handful of B's on their combined report cards and they have continued to excel, if not set the bar, in their graduate and post-graduate work.

Yes, I'm a proud Dad. That last paragraph is included for more than an excuse to brag. Looking at my daughters' achievements was also part of my journey with the Holy Spirit. I wondered why my girls were so motivated to excel. Sure, they were smart, well-adjusted, capable and confident young women (O.K., you're right. I'm bragging again). But could there have been another factor for their motivation to excel? Could I have communicated to them the same conditional love I felt from my father? Could their motive to succeed, in some measure, be an attempt to earn my approval?

All three girls played softball for several years. At one point, they were on three different teams. I can remember at least once when they played at different locations at the same time. It was a struggle to make sure everyone was at the right place at the right time. Parents, can I get an "Amen?" When our oldest became interested in trying softball (in addition to dance classes, church plays, swimming, and on and on), I thought it would be a good idea. The league was structured so that winning or losing was not the focus. The girls would learn the rules of the game, get some exercise and enjoy time with the other girls without a lot of pressure. That sounded like a great concept to me. I never excelled at sports, even though as a kid I enjoyed playing some sport every season. From football to basketball to baseball to swimming and skiing, I was always playing something. When time for the first softball game came around for my daughter, we loaded up the maroon minivan with fake wood paneling on the side and trooped out to the field.

"Play" is the operative word if you've ever seen young girls engage in their first ball game.

They play on the bench, talking and giggling while awaiting their turn at bat. They play in the dirt of the infield and play in the grass in the outfield. They play with their hats, their ball gloves and their hair. Sometimes they notice that they are part of something going on that has to do with a bat, a ball and bases, but only occasionally. It was my daughter's turn at bat. The ball was delivered in such a way that if they stuck out the bat, something good would happen. I was enjoying the low-key approach of the girls having a good time, until my girl got a hit. She started moving in the direction of first base, taking her time, enjoying the view and watching what the girls in the infield would do with the ball they had just picked up. She slowed her already slow pace about ten feet from first base while watching to see if she would get thrown out. By this time, I was shouting at her, "Run through the base, run through the base!" So much for my complicit observation of a little girl learning the game and enjoying the camaraderie! Another softball memory was much more painful.

As the Holy Spirit searched my heart about what kind of father I had been to my daughters, I had to acknowledge the possibility that some of the drive for achievement I saw in my daughters was a result of the expectations, weighty expectations, I had placed on them. I took the step from acknowledging the possibility, to actually accepting the responsibility for the unhealthy pressure to perform that I'm sure they felt. Even though I had overcome addictions, I still related to my daughters in ways my father had related to me and I'm sure his father to him. I asked my heavenly father to forgive me, and I knew I needed to ask for forgiveness from my daughters. I knew I had not expressed love and affirmation to them verbally. I had told them I loved them and had hugged them but not nearly enough. I knew I had missed some key moments to say, "It's alright. It doesn't matter. I love you." More than that, I knew there were times when I communicated displeasure to them at times when it was inappropriate, like times when they made a mistake or forgot something.

The Forgotten Glove

The Holy Spirit brought to my mind just such an incident that had left a deep sense of my displeasure and with it a deep scar. It was about a time when one of the girls forgot to bring her softball glove to a game. We lived across town from the softball field. It's not a big town, but it was about a fifteen-minute drive down back streets and cut-through roads. Our family is conscientious about getting to places on time. We're usually early and generally some of the first to arrive. So this day, we got to the ball field on time or maybe two or three minutes before. And then she realized that she had left her glove at home. That would mean 15 minutes home and fifteen minutes back. I was angry at my daughter for forgetting the glove and making us drive the round trip again. This time, I made the jaunt in record time. As a teenager I had a fast car and I learned to drive fast, too fast to be safe. I was driving faster than my little girl had ever experienced and it scared her. I'm sorry to admit that I knew she was scared, but I didn't slow down. We didn't talk either. This was her punishment for forgetting her glove. As I recall this incident, I am again embarrassed and ashamed that I let the situation get so out of hand. It really was no big deal, until in my selfishness and immaturity I made it a big deal. Her mistake didn't warrant this kind of response. I damaged her trust and security by my reaction.

I knew I needed to ask forgiveness for what I had done probably a decade earlier. I went to each of my daughters and confessed to them my shortcomings as a Dad the best I understood and in the best way that I could articulate them, asking for their forgiveness and prayer. With this daughter I asked, "Do you remember the night you forgot your softball glove?" She said, "Oh, yea! I remember." Regretfully, I knew she would. I asked for her forgiveness, expressing my love to her and praying together with her. With each of the girls, there were tears, hugs, heartfelt prayers and words of love. Now, I hug a lot more than I used to. I tell them I love them a lot more than I used to. I'm learning to be a Dad all over again, and by God's grace giving what I've received from my Abba.

The story of the Father's love is entwined with the acts of forgiveness. We have been forgiven through Jesus' death on the cross. We have been given grace to forgive those who have offended us or even despitefully used us. We can even find grace to ask forgiveness of those who we have wounded. There's grace to forgive. There's grace to begin again. There's grace for healing and restoration in the arms of Abba.

CHAPTER ELEVEN
THE FATHER WANTS HIS FAMILY BACK

Nancy and I were in a castle, also called a chateau, that had been renovated as a hotel in the French countryside. It was an idyllic setting. There were winding country roads inviting long walks or bicycle excursions through the fields of ripening sunflowers. The rooms had large windows overlooking what had once been an impressive estate. It was still impressive. And the meals…well it was in France, where dining is a national art form. The French don't eat. They dine. We were there as part of a team that had come to host a conference to encourage missionaries working in difficult places. Please suspend your skepticism about it being a hard place to minister. France, like most of the nations of Europe, is part of a post-Christian culture. People's hearts are generally closed to the gospel, so it's a very discouraging place for Christian outreach. We found that people in ministry in France live continually on the precipice of discouragement. Our team had come to bring a time of refreshing and mutual encouragement to these precious men and women who rarely got a break from the constant stress of cross-cultural ministry, living in an environment where they were met daily with rejection, if not ridicule. For them, the conference was a breath of fresh air. For us, it was a tough job, but somebody had to do it.

An Unforgettable Communion Service

Nancy and I have been a part of about a dozen of these "Operation Barnabas" conferences in Spain, France, Greece and Kazakhstan over the past 3 decades. I treasure special moments from many of these gatherings, and I know I'll never forget this one in France. Usually we would finish the conference on Saturday night with a communion service. Many of these services have been very touching. There has been forgiveness and reconciliation among the missionary community. Some have experienced a reconfirmation of their call to a nation, or a restoration of a vision, or a renewal in the call to ministry itself.

This time, Pastor Syvelle Phillips, a missionary statesman, was in France and had been invited by one of the missionaries to lead the communion service. It was a bit unusual for someone to lead the final evening who was not on the ministry team, but Pastor Phillips had come highly recommended. He had a lifetime of experience speaking to the hearts and hurts of missionaries, having endured many difficult battles himself. He spoke as a missions Father with a weight that pulled me in. He had an authority that comes from a lifetime of trusting God. I hung on every word. His eyes were full of the joy of salvation, yet at the same time piercing, seeing the work that was yet to be done, aware that there were fields white unto harvest. When he spoke about the cup and the loaf, the sacrifice of Jesus for the sins of the world, he came around to the same phrase again and again: "The Father wants his family back." These were not the words of a theologian parsing aspects of the atonement. They were the words of a man who had come to know the heart of the Father. He could say with authority and passion, "The Father wants his family back." Pastor Phillips had made difficult choice after difficult choice to hear the heartbeat of the Father and to give everything to live out the mandate of that cry. "The Father wants his family back." His words gave me a clear perception and a focused mission. My purpose in life is to join the Father in his pursuit to get his family back. It seemed so clear and powerful in its concentration, like a laser focusing energy in one spot. I also wanted to glean everything I could from Pastor Phillips, so I prayed, "Lord, I'd like to spend as much time as I can with this man." In the coming years, I would travel with Syvelle on my first trips to the continents of Africa and Asia.

As the Father heals and restores our hearts, we become more capable of knowing his heart. We live less and less out of our wounds and pain and live more and more in the life of the Spirit. In that life, we can feel a heart of compassion beating for every person. We can carry a longing for each person to experience the love of the heavenly Father. Jesus expressed the Father's heart of compassion when he looked upon the crowds of people and felt compassion for them. He saw the people like sheep without a shepherd, harassed and helpless, disoriented and defenseless, not knowing where to go or how to get there. As we know the Father, we can know his heart, like Jesus did. We, too, will have compassion for the crowds. We, too, will see their needs. Our cup is full. Our hearts are secure in love. We have what we need, but what about those who are harassed and helpless? Do you hear their cry?

Who Will Go?

Jeremiah's call to ministry happened before he was born. Before he was formed in his mother's womb, God called him as a prophet to the nations. If you read between the lines in Jeremiah, you get the sense that in Jeremiah's eyes, God had set him up in this prophet deal, and he wasn't too happy about it. He endured a lot of bad treatment because of his uninvited call as a prophet, and God was to blame for this fire in his bones.

Isaiah was different. He had this overwhelming experience of the holiness of God with angels, coals of fire, smoke, earthquakes and voices. He saw the Lord, then he heard the heart of the Lord. He heard a question voiced among the Trinity and that question expressed the heart of the Lord. "Whom shall I send and who will go for us?" Isaiah's famous answer (at least if you've heard a few missions messages) was, "Here am I. Send me!" Isaiah's call from here on out was a result of him hearing the Father's heart. Isaiah was intimate enough to hear and aligned with the Father's purpose enough to respond. And it wasn't going to be easy or go well from there. No matter, Isaiah had heard and responded because he knew the Father's heart, and the Father wanted his family back.

When I returned from Toronto back to my pastoral ministry in Arkansas, my prayer was, "Father, all I want is for the people in this church to know your love." I had been a person with large dreams. They were frustratingly unfulfilled, but I had always hoped for the big break. Now, I was content to live in Abba's love, to love others and to lead this small congregation of fewer than 100 to experience that same healing love. It was truly miraculous how the Spirit was poured out on us. Jesus was lifted up and we experienced the Father's love. Deep healing took place. People who had been abused as children forgave their earthly Fathers and were reconciled and set free. Father issues came to the surface, were confessed and freedom came.

For eight months, I preached on different aspects of the Father's love, and never came to the end of fresh insights in the Scriptures or new applications to life. But then something changed in my thinking. I was no longer content with the prospect of this congregation knowing the Father's love, wonderful as that was. I thought about those who didn't know this love. The multitudes, like the ones Jesus saw, who were harassed and helpless like sheep without a shepherd. It was not enough to confine my efforts to one precious congregation. Like Isaiah, I felt the Father's heart and heard his call. I grew in my awareness that the Father wanted his family back.

Ask of Me

I will proclaim the decree of the LORD: He said to me,
"You are my Son; today
I have become your Father.
Ask of me, and I will make the nations your inheritance,
the ends of the earth your possession. "

(Psalm 2:8-9)

This scripture passage has taken on fresh significance for me in understanding scripture in light of the Father/Son relationship. Surely, the words from the prophet Nathan (2 Samuel 7:14) were in David's mind as he wrote this prophetic Psalm. Seeing this Psalm through the lens of the New Testament, we can see it as a conversation between God, the Father, and God, the Son (Acts 13:33).

In this passage, the Father invites the Son to ask for the nations as his inheritance and the ends of the earth as his possession. This promise from the Father speaks of the same nations that Jesus focused on in his great commission (Matthew 28:18-20). He implored the disciples to make disciples of all nations. These are the same nations that are waiting to hear and receive the witness of this gospel of the kingdom (Matthew 24:14). These are the nations that will worship the Lamb that was slain throughout eternity. The nations are Jesus' inheritance from his Father. As co-heirs with Jesus, we are invited to share this inheritance with him. Paul's prayer for the Ephesian believers was that their eyes would be opened so they could see the riches of this inheritance in the saints, that is, that Jesus' rich inheritance is *us*, the saints, and those who believe through our witness. May the Holy Spirit open our eyes, too, to see this rich inheritance.

David presents a prophetic view of the inheritance of the nations by Jesus. The Apostle John provides a prophetic view of its fulfillment. Revelation 5:9 and 7:9 introduces parallel passages with a common element. They capture a scene of the Lamb of God at the throne. Creatures and elders sing a new song of praise to the Lamb "because you were slain and with your blood you purchased men for God from every tribe and language and people and nation." In chapter seven, the fulfillment is seen in this great uncountable multitude from every nation, tribe, people and language, crying out worship to the Lamb.

As sons and daughters of the Father, we've been invited to join the inheritance of the Only-Begotten. We've been commissioned by our elder brother to make disciples of all nations. We live in expectant hope that a day will come when compassion for the multitudes will culminate in songs of worship to the Son and to the Father, by the Spirit from every tribe and tongue and people and nation. There will be rejoicing throughout eternity because the Father will have his family back.

A Sinner Loved

Nancy and I had completed another Operation Barnabas Conference. We were invited to spend the weekend with one of the couples who attended the event before our flight back home. When we arrived at their home, we were introduced to the couple who had stayed with their children, so they could attend the conference. As we talked with the babysitters, an amazing story unfolded.

The wife grew up in a Muslim nation where there were few, if any, Christians. As a teenager the wife, we'll call her Natasha, got pregnant outside of marriage. Her infant daughter was taken from her. She was brought to the center of the village and savagely beaten with canes by the village elders. She showed us photos of the scars she still bears in her body. In addition, she was exiled to a remote island where her life was difficult. Before she went to the island, a Christian expat who was working in the nation gave her a copy of the New Testament. Another Christian ex-pat heard of her plight and would smuggle food to her under the cover of darkness. While on the island, Natasha had a lot of time to reflect on her situation. She considered reading the little book she had been given. Her thoughts went back and forth. If she read the Christian book, she would bring greater condemnation on herself from Allah. Then she reasoned, "I'm already going to hell for my sin. What difference does it make?"

So she began to read and in reading discovered a God who loves sinners.

She met a God who had come to her in her punishment, like a Father who would run to a rebellious son who had wasted everything. Natasha fell in love with the God who loves sinners. She found a Father who restored her as a precious daughter. The Christian man who smuggled food to her on the island found a way to smuggle her off the island and into another country. That man, a trained linguist, is now her husband. Natasha is one of the first believers from her nation and has given her life working to translate the scriptures (working with her husband) into her mother tongue so other sinners can know that God loves them. She wants her people to know that God is a loving Father who wants his family back.

The Story Ends Here: It's Your Turn

I find it ironic and even laughable that I would write a book about receiving and expressing love. I still think I'm not very good at expressing love. It's incomprehensible to me that I have experienced this powerful, intimate love of God as a Father. The Apostle Paul must have pondered this overwhelming realization as he prayed for the believers in Ephesus (Ephesians 3:17b-19).

And I pray that you, being rooted and established in love, may have power, together with all the saints, to grasp how wide and long and high and deep is the love of Christ, and to know this love that surpasses knowledge—that you may be filled to the measure of all the fullness of God.

When he wrote "to know this love that surpasses knowledge," maybe he had a smile on his face. You can try to know it and you should try to know it, and it's wide and long and deep, but I've got to tell you, children, it's beyond knowledge. Grasp what you can't grasp. Know what can't be known. Rationalize the supra-rational. Plumb the depths, explore the heights, but you'll never come to the end of it. You can be established in love. You can put your roots down deeply into love. But remember, you'll never understand the Father's love.

Live there. Receive and give love. Like a tiny minnow swimming in the vast ocean, there's always more. Always more.

In my experience of the Father's love, I've waited in his presence and felt his love pour into me more times than I can count. I've wept tears, moved by the sheer wonder of his love more times than I can number. I've watched and worshipped as Abba Father poured out his love on others in continent after continent, country after country, from Asia to Africa, from the Latin American south to the European north. I have seen the Father's love for his children.

I know that he loves you.

He waits to reveal his love to you and to embrace you as your Abba Father. Your Abba. Will you open your arms to embrace him as he runs to you? When the Father in Jesus' story embraced his son, he kissed him, too. Jesus was betrayed with a kiss, so that you could be restored with a kiss. In the horror of the cross was the hope that you would know the Father's love in the way that Jesus knew the Father's love. The Father is running to you with arms open wide. Will you open your arms to embrace him as he runs to you?

SUGGESTED BIBLIOGRAPHY

Arnott, John G., and Jack Frost. *Experiencing the Father's Embrace.* Shippensburg, PA: Destiny Image Publishers, Inc., 2002.

Bailey, Kenneth E. *Finding the Lost: Cultural Keys to Luke 15.* St. Louis: Concordia Publishing House, 1992.

_____. *Jesus Through Middle Eastern Eyes: Cultural Studies in the Gospels.* Downers Grove, IL: InterVarsity Press, 2008.

Eldridge, John. *Fathered by God: Learning What Your Dad Could Never Teach You.* Nashville: Thomas Nelson, Inc., 2009

_____. *Wild At Heart: Discovering the Secrets of A Man's Soul.* Nashville: Thomas Nelson, Inc., 2001, 2010

Manning, Brennan. *Abba's Child: The Cry of the Heart for Intimate Belonging.* Colorado Springs: Navpress, 2002.

_____. *Ruthless Trust: The Ragamuffin's Path to God.* New York: HarperCollins Publishers, 2002.

McClung, Floyd. *The Father Heart of God: Experiencing the Depth of His Love for You.* Eugene, OR: Harvest House Publishers, 1985.

Miller, Donald and John MacMurray. *To Own a Dragon: Reflections on Growing Up Without a Father.* Colorado Springs: NavPress, 2006.

Nouwen, Henri J.M. *Here and Now.* New York: Crossroads Publishing Co., 1994.

_____. *In the Name of Jesus* New York: Crossroad Publishing Co., 1989.

_____. *Life of the Beloved: Spiritual Living in a Secular World.* 2002

_____. *The Return of the Prodigal Son: A Story of Homecoming.* New York: Doubleday, 1992.

Piorek, Ed. *The Father Loves You.* Cape Town, South Africa: Vineyard International Publishing, 1999.

Stibbe, Mark. *From Orphans to Heirs: Celebrating our spiritual adoption.* Oxford: Bible Reading Fellowship, 2005.

Trent, John. *The Blessing: Giving the Gift of Unconditional Love and Acceptance.* Rev. ed. Nashville: Nelson, 2004.

Winter, Jack and Pamela Ferris. *The Homecoming: Unconditional Love: Finding Your Place in the Father's Heart.* Edmonds, WA: YWAM Publishing, 1999.